S268 Physical Resources and Environment

Science: a second level course

BUILDING MATERIALS

Prepared for the Course Team by Dave Williams

S268 Physical Resources and Environment

Course Team

Dave Williams (Course Chair)
Andrew Bell
Geoff Brown
Steve Drury
Chris Hawkesworth
Ian Nuttall (Editor)
Janice Robertson (Editor)
Peter Sheldon
Sandy Smith
Peter Webb
Chris Wilson
John Wright
Annemarie Hedges (Course Manager)
Charlie Bendall (Course Coordinator)

Production

Jane Sheppard (Graphic Designer)
Steve Best (Graphic Artist)
David Jackson (Series Producer, BBC)
Nicholas Watson (BBC Producer)
John Greenwood (Liaison Librarian)
Eira Parker (Course Secretary)
Marilyn Leggett (Secretary)
Lynn Tilbury (Secretary)

Course assessor

Professor Peter W. Scott, Camborne School of Mines.

Dedication

Professor Geoff Brown was a member of the Course Team when he was killed on the Galeras Volcano, Colombia, in January 1993. The Course Team dedicates S268 to his memory.

Acknowledgements

The Course Team gratefully acknowledges the contributions of members of the S238 course team (S238 The Earth's Physical Resources, 1984).

The Course Team also wishes to thank Sheila Dellow for careful reading of early drafts of the course material.

The Open University, Walton Hall, Milton Keynes MK7 6AA.

First published 1995. Reprinted (with corrections) 1998, 2002, 2003.

Edited, designed and typeset by The Open University.

Printed in the United Kingdom by Henry Ling Limited, at the Dorset Press, Dorchester, DT1 1HD.

ISBN 0 7492 5146 8

1.4

CONTENTS

1 INTRODUCTION

This Block is concerned with materials that are dug from the ground in vast quantities to be used for building and other construction purposes. It is not possible to be comprehensive and discuss all building materials, and so each Section concentrates on a major type of physical resource used in building.

Section 1 is an introduction to the present scale of building materials usage, and starts with some historical examples.

Section 2 explains how different rocks have been formed by the rock cycle, and the use of these rocks as building stones. Video Band 3: *Resource Geology* has already introduced typical rock types. The distribution and ages of the rocks of the UK are described via an explanation of the small *Postcard Geological Map* on Audio Band 2. Video Band 4: *Stones for Building* shows something of the variety of natural building stones in use today. You will be able to examine samples of typical building materials in the Rock Kit; these are described on Audio Band 3.

Section 3 discusses the simplest of all the naturally occurring bulk materials, sands and gravels, which have been used in ever-increasing quantities over the last hundred years, particularly in concrete.

Section 4 is about clays and clay minerals, and their use to make bricks and tiles.

Section 5 discusses limestones, and particularly their use for making cement, the main ingredient of mortar and concrete.

Section 6 is concerned with gypsum and other minerals formed by the large-scale evaporation of seawater.

Section 7 considers aggregates made by crushing hard rocks; these are used in huge quantities in a modern industrial society, mainly for high-strength concrete, and particularly for road-making. Simple tests are used to assess the suitability of the Kit rocks as road materials, which is discussed in Audio Band 4. The interplay between aggregates (which account for over a third of all quarried rock in the UK) and transport is investigated in Video Band 5: *Rocks for Roads*, by looking at some of the problems of aggregate supply.

This leads finally to Section 8, where the issues of planning and the development of building resources in the future are discussed in a wider context. Huge quantities of building materials are still needed now and in the future, so the questions of how their supply is to be organized, where new large quarries are to be sited, and how they are to be made environmentally acceptable, are key issues which are likely to be actively debated for years to come. Controversy about transport — today focused on roads and the materials to build them — is not new. Victorian opposition to the railways — 'snorting steam monsters' cutting across the countryside, though allowing new travel opportunities to many — made them unpopular in many quarters.

In the early 1990s the amount of material used in the UK for building and road-making is running at 250–300 million tonnes a year, a figure typical for an industrialized country. This dwarfs the activities of all the other extractive industries, especially coal, for which output had fallen in the early 1990s to less than 40 million tonnes a year, and the mining of metal ores, important in Britain since Roman times, has virtually ceased. Building materials amount to an annual turnover of well over a billion pounds sterling ($£10^9$) in the UK, compared with a few million pounds for metal ores. The main environmental effects of the building materials industry are large holes left in the ground.

Building materials are cheap compared with other physical resources, and so supplies have traditionally been sought locally, because the cost of transport can easily exceed the cost of extraction. This Block is concerned with large tonnages, at low cost per tonne, a situation you will meet again with water in Block 3. Later in the Course, when we consider fuels and metals, the costs per tonne are much higher, and so transport costs are less critical. However, small quantities of ornamental rocks for specialized use have always been carried long distances, since their higher value can bear the costs of carriage.

In this Block we shall not discuss several important materials used in today's buildings: wood is a biological rather than a physical resource; steel and aluminium are metals (Block 5), and there are specialized materials such as glass and plastics, which have many other uses and form only a small part of the fabric of buildings. On the other hand, we shall mention several things that are not strictly 'building materials', such as the environmental issues associated with the quarries from which building materials have been extracted, and the use and disposal of wastes, which are often tipped into these same quarries.

1.1 History of building materials

You have already seen in Block 1 that in Palaeolithic times (the Old Stone Age — up to about 8 000 years ago in Britain) early Man used volcanic glass and flint for tools in place of wood and bone. Probably the first materials used for primitive homes were organic materials; wood and thatch are still sufficient for houses in some places today (such as the Hadareb house, Figure 9, Block 1). But stone and brick make more permanent houses, and important structures have always been constructed from the most durable materials available. Humans have been using stone for building for many centuries; in the UK the remains of Neolithic stone buildings, dating from about 6000BC, can be seen in the Orkneys.

Natural stone has been quarried and shaped to form blocks for buildings and walls for thousands of years, and stones have also often been elaborately carved for decorating buildings. A recurring theme in the study of building materials is the interplay between physical properties and appearance. Humans have always valued the appearance of their houses; they have laid even greater stress on the design of important buildings for meetings or business, especially ones that have ceremonial significance (Figure 1). There has been a long history of very sophisticated building using natural stone, as indicated by the examples in the boxes 'Building the Cheops Pyramid' and 'The Romans as builders'.

Even the Roman walls and roads pale besides the 2 000 km of the Great Wall of China, built about 200BC, and the Inca road through Peru, which runs some 6 000 km from Ecuador to central Chile, and was built over 1 000 years ago.

Sun-dried bricks were used in hot climates at least 3 000 years ago, for example in the Middle East and India; later the Romans produced good fired bricks, tiles and pipes, made from the many different types of local clay which they found all across northern Europe.

Prodigious efforts were involved in the elaborate design and delicate masonry in cathedrals built in the Middle Ages. Durham Cathedral, for example, is very large: it required the preparation of about 100 000 tonnes of carefully shaped blocks of masonry and took several decades to complete. It has since been added to and refurbished over the centuries.

(b)

(a)

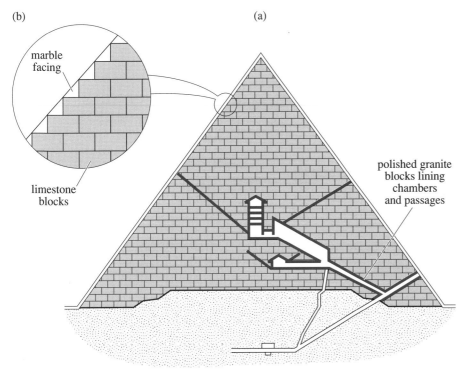

marble facing

limestone blocks

polished granite blocks lining chambers and passages

Figure 1 The Cheops Pyramid at Giza, near Cairo, Egypt: (a) sectional view, showing internal chambers and passages, many of which are lined with granite; (b) sectional view to show sloping marble facing on rectangular limestone blocks; (c) extraction techniques in the quarries.

(c)

Building the Cheops Pyramid

The great pyramid at Giza (Plate 8) is one of many complex structures erected in Egypt over 4 500 years ago, and has the following statistics:

size of pyramid base: 230 m × 230 m

height: 140 m

size of blocks: about 1 m³ (1 cubic metre)

workforce: about 10 000, probably in small gangs

construction time: about 30 years

○ How many blocks would have been needed to build this pyramid? (The volume of a pyramid is given by: area of base × $\frac{1}{3}$ height.)

○ Volume = 230 × 230 × 140/3
= 2 468 700 m³

As the volume of one block is one cubic metre, about 2.5 million blocks would have been needed.

It is difficult to comprehend the effort involved in the construction of the ancient Egyptian pyramids. The pyramid of Cheops at Giza is the biggest, and even today is probably still the largest **masonry** structure ever built. (A masonry structure is one made of natural stone, trimmed into regularly shaped blocks.) The bulk of the rock came from quarries within a few hundred metres of the site, and is a fairly soft limestone, which could relatively easily be **dressed** (chiseled) by simple tools. Consider some of the logistics involved.

○ How many tonnes of stone must have been quarried to build this pyramid? (A cubic metre of limestone weighs about 2.5 t; assume 30% wastage for trimming and squaring the blocks.)

○ Weight of stone quarried = volume of pyramid × density of stone × wastage factor

$\approx (2.5 \times 10^6 \times 2.5 \times 130/100)$ tonnes

≈ 8.1 million tonnes

○ If each gang had 8 people, and they quarried, dressed and placed their own blocks on the pyramid (just possible, since the quarries were close), how many blocks would each gang have to put in place each week?

○ Number of weeks available in 30 years: 30 × 52 = 1 560.

Number of gangs: 10 000/8 = 1 250.

Therefore number of 'gang-weeks'
= 1 560 × 1 250 = 1 950 000

and number of blocks per gang per week

$= \frac{2\,500\,000}{1\,950\,000} \approx 1.3$

So each gang of eight would have to average just over one block a week. Almost as striking as this effort is the organization of food, etc., to support such a huge workforce, and the design and coordination of the construction itself.

These large blocks of limestone were prepared and erected with phenomenal accuracy to form such a huge structure, which had to be regular, square and level to within a few centimetres. (The sides of the pyramid run north–south, east–west to within about 1/30th of a degree.) Also, at least some of the joints between blocks are so well made that a knife blade can only just be put between them. So the blocks must have been very carefully dressed square and rubbed flat. The present stepped appearance is because the original smooth surface layer of tapered marble blocks has been removed, together with many limestone blocks, and re-used in more recent buildings in nearby Cairo. This is probably one of the earliest examples of the *recycling* of building stone. Less effort is needed to remove dressed blocks from an existing masonry structure than to cut new stone from the quarry.

Most of the pyramid is made of cubes of local limestone, but the corridors and the roofs of the burial chambers are lined with exactly square, huge smoothed beams and slabs of granite. These weigh up to 50 tonnes, and are positioned up to 100 metres above the desert floor. The use of this granite was a remarkable feat: it was quarried 500 miles away, and the blocks were then shipped down the Nile. Granite is a very hard rock, and so much more difficult to dress to shape than limestone. Hand rubbing must have been an extremely laborious way of preparing smooth surfaces on these huge granite blocks.

The Romans as builders

The Romans too were master builders, and erected a great number of sophisticated civil engineering structures, many of them still standing. Figure 2a shows an aqueduct in Segovia, Spain, built of local granite. This aqueduct, which has 165 arches and is nearly 30 m high, was in more or less continuous use for nearly 2 000 years, but recent air pollution is now seriously attacking the granite.

For more important ceremonial buildings in Rome, they shipped stone for special uses many hundreds of kilometres from the outposts of the empire (Figure 2b). The pillars and columns of the Pantheon temple (Plate 9) are made of single pieces of stone, about 1.5 m in diameter and nearly 12 m high, from Mons Claudianus in the Egyptian Eastern Desert. In other buildings in Rome some single columns of this stone are almost 2 m in diameter and 18 m in height. The

Mons Claudianus quarry lies more than 100 km east of the Nile, so that for the initial part of the journey columns weighing about 100 tonnes had to be carried across the desert.

The Romans also prepared excellent cement, with which they were able to construct large concrete structures; for example, the Pantheon is capped by a 43 m diameter concrete dome. This dome was the largest in the world for about 1 500 years before St Paul's, London, was built by Christopher Wren. (After the fall of the Roman Empire, cement and concrete technologies were lost and not rediscovered until the eighteenth century.) The Romans were also great road and wall builders; for example, much of Hadrian's wall, which once linked Newcastle upon Tyne with the Solway estuary, still stands.

Figure 2 (a) Roman aqueduct at Segovia in Spain, built of local granite in the first century and still in use in the 1960s.

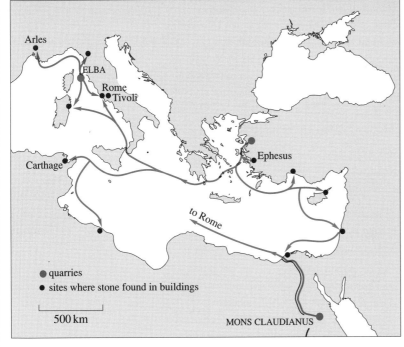

(b) Map of Roman granite imports for ceremonial buildings, first to fifth centuries AD.

The main lesson to be learned from study of the work of early builders such as the Romans is that for large structures it is best to use local materials wherever possible to minimize transport costs. Stone with special properties, such as a particularly attractive appearance, and stone that is easily carved and yet resistant to the weather, has always been highly valued, and so is worth transporting long distances, especially if it can be brought by ship. These criteria remain equally valid today for modern buildings.

1.2 Building materials today

The modern equivalent of the major construction projects of the Ancient World might be the dramatic sweep of the concrete 'sails' of the Sydney Opera House, or the large-scale engineering works of the Dover-to-Calais channel tunnel.

The basic ingredients and technology of most building materials have been well established for a very long time. Today, surface treatment by mechanical cutting and polishing enables large sheets of granite and marble to be prepared for cladding the outside of shops, offices and, particularly, banks, to provide an attractive natural stone 'skin' covering a much cheaper wall. Also the traditional building materials — stone, brick, concrete and wood — are still used, but are now combined with others, such as steel, glass, plastics and plasterboard. Cut and dressed (masonry) stone amounts to only a small fraction of the building material used today, probably only about 1 million tonnes per year in the UK, out of an EU total of 16 million tonnes.

Almost anywhere on Earth, building materials of some kind can be found just below the surface. Many materials used for building are made from either sands, gravels or clays, which can be found lying loose on top of the solid bedrock. In the UK much of this material has been deposited during the last 50 000 years, towards the end of, or since, the last glacial period, when huge amounts of rock fragments, sands and clays were deposited along the edge of the melting ice which covered much of Britain. (This is discussed in Section 3.2.)

In an industrialized society like the UK, there is a need for huge amounts of cheap building materials, especially for roads and buildings, and these loose surface materials (which can be easily excavated with modern machinery) have been widely exploited. In the UK today about 100 million tonnes of sand and gravel are dug out each year, much of it being used more or less as extracted as cheap 'fill' or mixed with cement to make concrete. Even larger amounts of hard rocks, mainly limestones and igneous rocks, are quarried and crushed to form **aggregate**, also used chiefly in concrete, and for road-making. Together these two sources account for most of the annual production in the UK of over 250 million tonnes of building materials.

However, world wide it has been estimated that each year in the early 1990s about 11 billion tonnes (11×10^9 t) of solid rock, much of it dressed for building stone, is being worked, and about 9 billion tonnes of sands and gravels are extracted.

○ If the extraction of the main raw materials (sands, gravels and crushed rocks) for use in the UK building industry today generates about £1.5 billion per year, what is the average price per tonne?

○ If 250 million tonnes have a total value of about a £1.5 billion, the average price is about £6 per tonne. This is the price as extracted at the quarry. Value can be added to these raw materials by making products like ready-mix concrete or cement blocks.

For many of the resources discussed in this Course their *chemical composition* is vital: you cannot extract a metal from an ore unless the metal is there in the first place! But for many building materials, it is their *physical and mechanical* properties which are most important. For example, materials for road-making must have a high crushing strength, and for materials to be used on the outside of buildings, appearance and resistance to the weather are important.

Another feature of building materials separates them from many other resources in this Course: most of the material dug from the ground is actually used, so that even when any waste has been returned to the quarry, a large hole remains. The main long-term environmental effects of the extraction of building materials relate to these large holes, and their subsequent use. Abandoned 'dry' quarries may be valuable as sites for waste disposal, but old quarries dug below the natural level of water in the ground fill with water to make artificial lakes, often used by wildlife or for leisure.

Question 1

(a)   What was the approximate production per capita of building materials in the UK in the early 1990s?

(b)   How does this compare with the world's per capita production of building materials?

1.3   Summary of Section 1

1   Stone and other building materials have been used for many thousands of years, hand crafted to make large and complex masonry structures. Only building stone with unusual properties has ever been worth transporting long distances.

2   Today in industrialized societies, the large-scale extraction of low-value building materials dominates the industry, leaving large holes in the ground. Materials are usually extracted as close as possible to where they are used in order to minimize transport costs.

3   Physical and mechanical properties, rather than chemical properties, are the most important features of many building materials.

2 BUILDING STONES

2.1 The rock cycle and building materials

You were introduced to the rock cycle in Section 3.5 of Block 1 (Figure 60); in this Section we shall look in more detail at the rock cycle and materials for the building industry, particularly building stones. Figure 3 shows schematically where some of the common building materials are formed in terms of the rock cycle of igneous, sedimentary and metamorphic rocks.

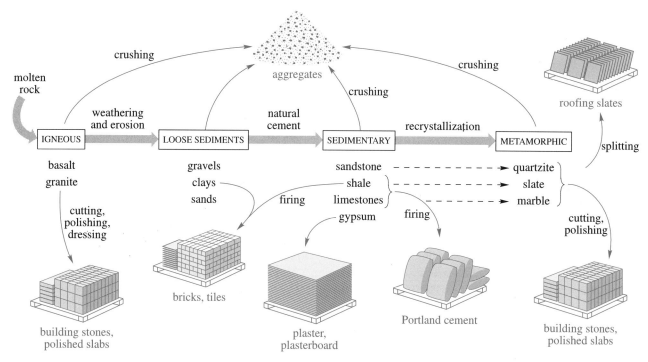

Figure 3 Building materials and the rock cycle. The Figure shows, from left to right in boxes, the three classes of rocks — igneous, sedimentary and metamorphic; typical rocks are named below. All rocks can be weathered and eroded to form loose clastic sediments on the Earth's surface: sands and gravels (Section 3), and clays (Section 4). Soluble material from weathering goes into the sea to eventually form the chemical sediments: limestones (Section 5) and evaporites such as gypsum (Section 6). Crushed aggregates (Section 7) can be made from any tough rock. Processes are indicated by coloured arrows, and building industry products are shown on pallets.

This Section is concerned with rocks after they have been buried and cemented to form a hard sedimentary rock, and heated at high pressure by deeper burial to recrystallize as metamorphic rocks, or melted to form igneous rocks. The main purpose here is to show how different types of building stones are formed, and how they can be described and related to their origin. Most types of rock have been used somewhere for building, and their distri-bution across the country has had a considerable influence both on the buildings seen today and the building resources which are available to be extracted. The *Postcard Geological Map* (Section 2.4) will help to explain this distribution.

2.2 The rock cycle and sedimentary rocks

Most of the mineral and rock fragments produced by weathering and erosion at the Earth's surface will form muds, sands and gravels, which are carried away by rivers towards the sea, to be eventually laid down in layers. In time the layers become consolidated to form fragmental or clastic sedimentary rocks — that is, rocks made of fragments of earlier rocks.

● Would you expect a fast-flowing river to deposit coarser-grained sand than a slower-moving one?

○ The faster the current, the larger the sediment size that can be transported, and so the faster river would deposit the coarser sediment.

In general, the faster that water is flowing (that is, the *higher the energy* of the transporting medium) the *larger* the particles of sediment that the water is able to move. Small fragments of clay and silt are easily caught up in the flowing water and carried along in **suspension**. Larger particles of sand and gravel will roll or bounce along the bottom of the stream, a process that tends to abrade the transported particles and reduce them in size. Thus, in steep, fast mountain streams, many pebbles and even boulders are tumbled along in the vigorous waters. In the lower, flatter reaches of river valleys, muds and clays form most of the sediment carried along in the slow-moving, *lower-energy environment*.

Most of this finer sediment, mainly sands and clays, will sooner or later reach the sea, where it may be mixed with coarser beach deposits eroded from the cliffs. Eventually all this sediment from the land will be deposited as layers of pebbles, sand and clay on the sea floor.

2.2.1 Sorting of sediments

As sedimentary materials are transported and deposited, usually by water, there is a tendency for the particles to be selected into different sizes, both during transport, and at the time of deposition. The degree of **sorting** is determined partially by the distance and length of time that particles have been in transport, and partly by the conditions where they are eventually deposited. (The greater the time and distance travelled, and the more even the conditions in the environment of deposition, the better sorted the sediment will be.) A well-sorted sediment will tend to contain grains of a similar size (Figure 4a), as might result from a long period of gentle washing back and forth of low-energy waves on a beach.

A poorly sorted sediment is one in which grains of various sizes are jumbled together. This tends to happen when sediments have been swiftly transported over short distances, and rapidly deposited in variable conditions, for example in streams or rivers that are subject to large fluctuations in energy due to seasonal variations in flow. Such a poorly sorted material is shown in Figure 4b. These differences in degree of sorting can be shown by sieving the sediments into their different size fractions, and then plotting the weight of each size as a **histogram**; the narrower the histogram, the better the sorting (Figure 4c). Alternatively, a **cumulative frequency curve** can be used, where the distribution of grain sizes from the histogram is drawn as a single curve from 0% to 100% (Figure 4e).

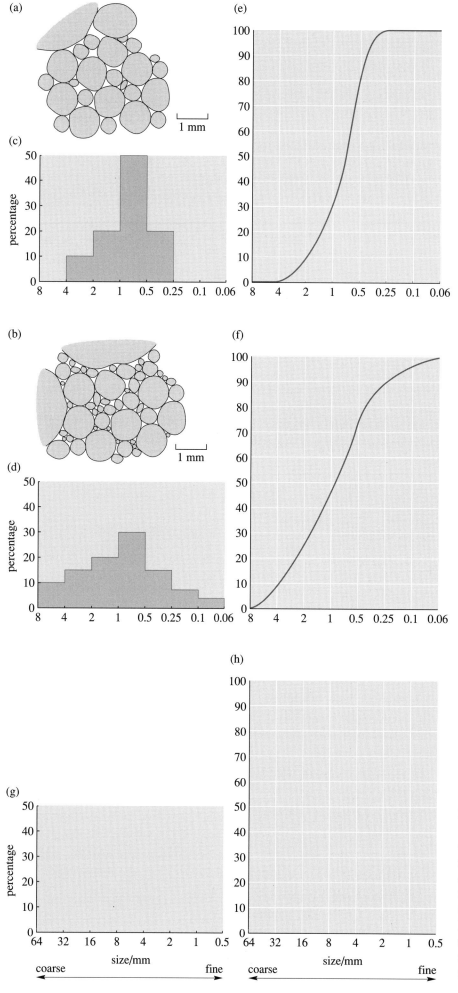

Figure 4 Well-sorted and poorly sorted sands: (a) sketch of well-sorted sand, where most of the grains are of similar sizes, with a lot of pore space between the grains; (b) sketch of poorly sorted sand, where grains of a mixture of sizes pack well together, so its porosity is much less; (c) histogram and (e) cumulative frequency curve of the well-sorted sand; (d) histogram and (f) cumulative frequency curve of the poorly sorted sand (well-sorted materials have narrow histograms with a high peak and steep cumulative frequency curves, whereas poorly sorted materials have broad histograms and less steep cumulative frequency curves); (g) and (h) for use with Question 2. In parts (c) to (h) the vertical scale is in weight per cent and the horizontal scale is in millimetres.

When plotting sediment sizes, by convention, both histograms and cumulative frequency curves are drawn as in Figure 4, with the coarsest grain size shown on the *left*, and with the grains getting 50% smaller for each mark to the right on the horizontal axis of the graph. This corresponds to the sequence of sizes passing down a normal stack of sieves. Any point on a cumulative frequency curve shows the weight percentage of all the grains having a diameter larger than that size, read off the horizontal axis.

The size distribution of many industrial materials is often plotted in a similar way as a histogram or cumulative frequency curve, because the properties of many materials can vary widely with their degree of sorting, and the differences show up well on these diagrams. For example, it is easy to see the predominant grain size of a sample from the position of the 'peak' of the histogram, and to compare several samples by plotting their cumulative frequency curves on the same graph.

⬤ You have been given sieving data from another sand, which is slightly better sorted the one shown in Figure 4b. Will it plot as a shallower- or steeper-slope cumulative frequency curve than the one in Figure 4f?

◯ If it is better sorted than the sand in Figure 4b, it will plot as a *steeper* slope than Figure 4f — that is, more like the sand in Figure 4a, whose cumulative frequency curve is shown as Figure 4e.

2.2.2 *Porosity*

Porosity is a measure of the space between the grains in a rock or between the particles in an artificial building material like concrete. It is normally expressed as a percentage of the total volume of the material:

$$\text{porosity} = \frac{\text{volume of space}}{\text{total volume}} \times 100\%$$

Porosity in rocks is important for two main reasons:

• The pores are where water, oil or gas can be stored, so determining the amount of these important fluids that can be held in the rock to form a reservoir.

• The pores are where mineral cement forms between the grains to turn a loose sediment into a sedimentary rock.

Of course, no natural collection of grains will be all exactly the same size, or perfectly spherical.

⬤ Will perfect spheres have a higher or lower porosity than irregular grains?

◯ Irregular grains will tend to fit together better than perfect spheres, and so have a *lower* porosity.

⬤ Will a rock with a range of grain sizes have a lower or higher porosity than one with a single grain size?

◯ A mixture of grain sizes will fit together better than grains of a single size. Smaller grains can fit between the larger ones, and so a rock with grains of several sizes will have a lower porosity than one with a single grain size (compare Figures 4a and 4b).

What controls the amount of porosity in a sediment? It is easiest to start by considering how grains can be packed together (see box overleaf).

Theoretical close-packing of spheres and porosity

Imagine 2 cm cubes regularly stacked together so that there are no spaces between them. Each cube is then removed from the stack and has its corners rounded off to become a perfect sphere of 2 cm diameter (1 cm radius) before being put back exactly where it came from. There would now be an unstable stack of spheres, where each one just touched six others, with a large amount of pore space between the spheres. Such a 'rock' would have a very high porosity (Figure 5a).

● What percentage of the original material has been removed? This will be the maximum porosity of a sediment made of equal-sized spherical grains stacked in this way.

● volume of each original cube

= 2 × 2 × 2 = 8 cubic centimetres (cm³)

volume of each sphere

$$= \frac{4}{3}\pi r^3 = \frac{4}{3} \times \frac{22}{7} \times 1^3 = 4.19 \, cm^3$$

volume of material removed from each cube

= 8 − 4.19 = 3.81 cm³

The porosity = 3.81/8 × 100% = 47.6% (see Figure 5a).

A practical demonstration of the situation in Figure 5a could be achieved by packing a box with open vertical tubes of tennis balls, such that the rows of tubes are all aligned; the diagram shows the view from above the box. A porosity of 47.6% would then be achieved no matter how many balls are in the tubes, because the balls in one layer are exactly above those in the layer below, and the balls in one vertical plane are all lined up horizontally with balls in adjacent planes. In this situation each ball in the body of the box is surrounded by six others.

If we then move alternate rows of tubes half a tube width sideways, we should then have the two-dimensional close-packed arrangement shown in Figure 5b, where again we are looking at the box from above. Each tube of balls is now in contact with two tubes in the adjacent rows, and each ball in the body of the box is surrounded by eight others.

The closest packing is shown in Figure 5c. This arrangement is achieved by removing the tubes, so that all the balls in one layer lie in the hollows between the balls in the layer below. Each ball will now be surrounded by twelve others, six in its own layer and three each in the layer above and the layer below. This is the way spherical grains tend to arrange themselves in natural sediments, with a porosity of 26%.

(a)　　　　　　　　　(b)　　　　　　　　　(c)

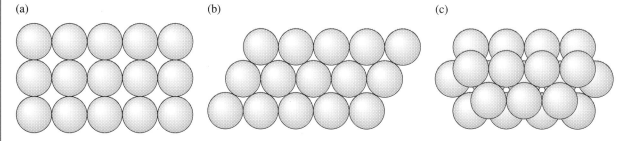

Figure 5 Diagram to show how spherical grains can be stacked together to leave different spaces (porosity) between them: (a) plan view of loose packing — rows of spheres exactly above the one below (highest porosity); (b) close-packing in two dimensions (view from above); (c) close-packing in three dimensions (porosity 26%).

Activity 1 Packing pickles into a jar (making a low-porosity sediment)

How does the porosity decrease as a mixtures of different-sized spheres are packed together into a container, and what is the minimum pore space achievable?

Packing pickled onions, etc., into a jar, is a useful analogy. Table 1 gives the amount of water (in cm³) needed to fill the same 70 mm diameter, 700 cm³ capacity pickle jar to the brim, when packed with mixtures of different-sized materials; onions, peas and rice represent different grain sizes in a sediment.

You may like to try this Activity for yourself; similar harmless kitchen materials such as cut-up carrots, potatoes and other vegetables would be equally suitable. You should avoid materials that absorb significant amounts of water, since they would give you a false indication of the pore volume. The aim is to get the porosity below 10%, to simulate a good low-porosity rock. (It is not strictly necessary for you to do the Activity, provided you can do Question 2.)

The method is simple: fill the jar with materials, and then top up with water. Pour off the liquid into a kitchen jug calibrated in cm^3 to measure the porosity between the 'grains'. Column 1 shows that there was about 46% of the space filled with vinegar when only 30 mm diameter onions were in the jar from the shop. In the next experiment we did, the porosity fell to 29% when a mixture of 30 mm and 14 mm diameter onions was used (column 2). When we included some 7.5 mm diameter peas in addition (column 3), the porosity fell to 26%, and finally, with a mixture that had 3 mm-diameter rice added and the jar shaken (column 5), the porosity fell to less than 14%.

Table 1 Onions, peas and rice grains in a 700 cm^3 jar

	Column	1	2	3	4	5
Row	Materials in jar	30 mm onions	30 mm and 14 mm onions	As column 2 + 7.5 mm peas	As column 3 + 3 mm rice	As column 4, but shaken
1	capacity of jar/cm^3	700	700	700	700	700
2	volume of water added/cm^3	320	205	180	120	95
3	∴ volume of solids/cm^3	380	495	520	580	605
4	pore space/%	45.7	29.3	25.7	17.1	13.6

It would have been possible to reduce the porosity further by adding smaller materials than rice to fill up the pore spaces between the rice grains.

Finally, we collected all the solid contents in column 5 in Table 1 and measured the volumes of each material (Table 2). Their combined volume agreed with that derived in row 3 of Table 1. You can now calculate the size distribution of the different-sized materials in this artificial sediment from row 2 in Table 2.

Table 2 Amounts of solid materials in jar (from column 5, Table 1)

Row	Materials	30 mm onions	14 mm onions	7.5 mm peas	3 mm rice
1	number	8	104	450	5 440
2	volume/cm^3	210	175	120	100
3	total volume of solids/cm^3	605	605	605	605
4	volume, as % of total volume of solids	35			

Question 2

Table 2, row 2 gives the volumes of the different particle sizes in the filled pickle jar, from column 5, Table 1.

(a) Complete Table 2, and then plot these results as a histogram on Figure 4g and as a cumulative frequency curve on Figure 4h.

(b) Is the material in the jar coarser- or finer-grained than the sediment plotted in Figure 4d and f?

(c) Is the material in the jar better sorted than the sediment plotted in Figure 4d and f?

Under natural conditions the *best* sorting of grain sizes occurs when a steady wind blows sand grains across a desert: grains too large to be rolled by the wind are left behind, and fine dust blows away completely, leaving well-rounded sand grains all of a similar size (see Figure 6a). When these grains are cemented together, a well-sorted sandstone is formed (see Figure 6d).

The *poorest* sorting occurs in nature when material is left behind by a melting glacier. Large boulders can be carried on or inside a glacier, whereas rocks frozen into the bottom of the ice are ground down to a fine 'rock flour'. If the ice melts rapidly all these grain sizes can be 'dumped' together to form a badly sorted sediment, called **till**, or **boulder clay**, which is a complete mixture of all grain sizes from clays to boulders.

2.2.3 *From loose sediments to sedimentary rocks*

Two processes are involved in transforming a loose sediment into a sedimentary rock. **Compaction** occurs as loose sediments become buried, and so, subjected to the weight of later overlying sediments, the mineral grains are forced closer together, and water is expelled. **Cementation** occurs as minerals are deposited in the pores of loose sediments by percolating water; this binds the mineral grains together to form a hard rock. The most common cementing minerals are calcite (calcium carbonate, $CaCO_3$) and quartz (silica, SiO_2).

In the formation of finer-grained sedimentary rocks, silts and clays, cementation is less important than compaction and the expulsion of water. The small flake-like particles of clay minerals tend to line up with each other during compaction, and a lot of water is expelled as the rock shrinks and becomes denser (Figure 6e). Coarser sediments, such as sands and gravels, suffer very little compaction and water loss when they are compressed at depth because the quartz grains are already closely packed in loose sand, and cannot be further compressed (Figure 6b). Here the main process is cementation (Figure 6b, c and d), and sandstones well cemented by quartz can be very strong.

Activity 2 *From loose sediment to sedimentary rock — an experiment with sugar*

A useful analogy for the cementation of loose sand to form sandstone can be made with sugar. Dry sugar behaves just like sand, and sugar cubes are similar to cemented sandstone. Add a few drops of water to a bowl of sugar and then allow them to dry thoroughly over several hours.

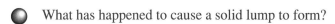 What has happened to cause a solid lump to form?

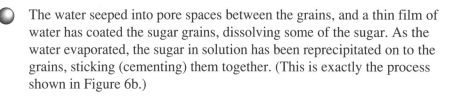 The water seeped into pore spaces between the grains, and a thin film of water has coated the sugar grains, dissolving some of the sugar. As the water evaporated, the sugar in solution has been reprecipitated on to the grains, sticking (cementing) them together. (This is exactly the process shown in Figure 6b.)

The 'experiment' works the other way around as an analogy of the weathering of a building stone with a soluble cement like calcite by acid rainwater. A few drops of water added to a sugar cube, quickly 'run through' the pores between the grains of the cube, showing that it is porous (seen more clearly with coloured water). Soon, sufficient sugar has dissolved for the cube to crumble under its own weight, because the 'cement' sticking the individual grains together has been dissolved. In the same way, mediaeval cathedrals built of limestone are today crumbling after prolonged exposure to acid rain. (Sugar is

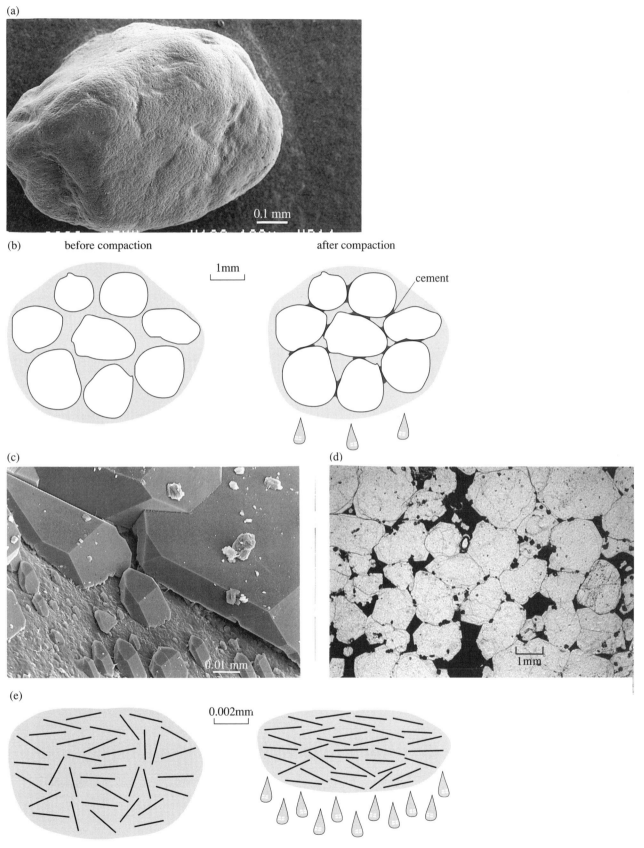

Figure 6 From loose sediment to sedimentary rock: (a) Sand grain from the Saudi Arabian desert, well rounded by grain-to-grain contacts (sand blasting). (b) From sand to sandstone (cementation): the grains of quartz were supporting each other in the loose sand, and only squash down a little due to the weight of overlying rocks. Grains become attached to each other as quartz cement is deposited between the grains, some of this cement having come from dissolving of the grains where they touch, a process known as pressure solution. (c) Aligned quartz crystals growing as a cement coating on the rough surface of a sandstone grain. (d) Cemented sandstone formed from quartz grains in part c. (e) From clay to mudstone (compaction): the small flakes of clay minerals here are originally almost 'floating' in water. As compaction proceeds, they become squashed together, thus expelling a lot of water, and become lined up to be nearly parallel to each other by the time the original mud has become a mudstone or shale. Very little in the way of mineral cement is deposited here.

so much more soluble in water than common rock-forming minerals that this weathering analogy is inappropriate if more than a trace of water is used.)

2.2.4 Grain size and minerals in sedimentary rocks

Figure 7 shows the terms used to describe grain sizes in sediments. The horizontal scale is the same as Figure 4: each interval on the scale decreases to the right by half, so it is a logarithmic scale. It is useful to know the terms used for the various grain sizes of loose sediments:

clay: < 0.002 mm; invisible under the microscope, feels smooth between the teeth

silt: 0.002–0.06 mm; too small to see, but 'gritty' to the teeth, like toothpaste

sand: 0.06–2 mm; can be seen with the naked eye, and feels gritty between the fingers

pebble: 4–60 mm (pea to cricket ball)

cobble   60–200 mm

boulder: >200 mm (bigger than a football)

('gravel' is a term applied to any loose sediment coarser than sand.)

At the bottom of the grain size diagram in Figure 7, the names of sedimentary rocks and their main minerals are given. It is clear that the processes that transport and deposit sediments not only sort out materials by size, but also tend to separate grains of *different minerals*. The coarsest sedimentary rocks, conglomerates, are made up of broken fragments (pebbles) of rocks; sandstones are usually formed mainly of grains of the mineral quartz; mudstones and shales have a large amount of clay minerals. Flakes of mica are most abundant in fine sands and silts.

Mudstones cannot be used for building because they are very poorly cemented. They tend to swell and crumble when exposed to the weather, since the clay minerals present re-absorb water (the reverse of the process shown in Figure 6e). Clays are, however, a vital source of material for brick-making

Figure 7 Classification of loose sediment (top), and sedimentary rock (bottom), by grain size. Silt is intermediate in grain size between sand and clay, and the terms 'mud', 'mudstone' and 'shale' apply to mixtures of silts and clays. The coloured boxes at the bottom show the size ranges of common sedimentary minerals. Of course, many sedimentary rocks contain mixtures of these grain sizes; for example, conglomerates are often 'pebbly sandstones'.

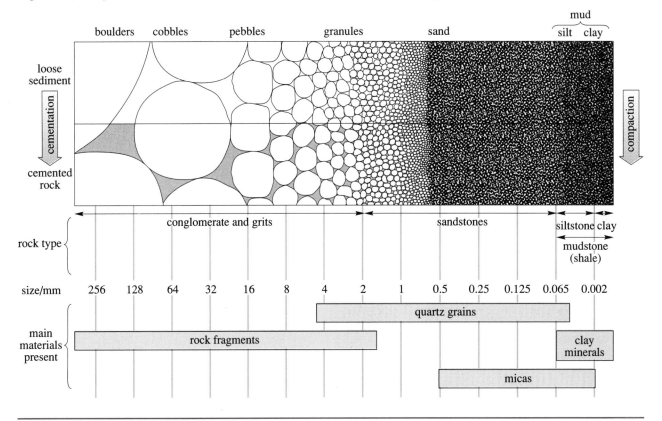

and have been the traditional building material in areas where there are no rocks suitable for building stone.

Most of the traditional building stones used in the UK are sedimentary rocks, well-cemented limestones and sandstones, whose porosity is not very high. They usually occur in horizontal or gently inclined layers or beds, and can be easily quarried.

2.3 The rock cycle; igneous and metamorphic rocks

Igneous and metamorphic rocks are generally hard and crystalline, and are usually more resistant to weathering and erosion than sedimentary rocks. They are common in Scotland, Wales and Northern Ireland, but are much scarcer in southern England, as we shall see in Section 2.4.

Igneous rocks have developed a very strong network of mineral grains which 'grew into' each other as the molten rock crystallized on cooling. Consequently, they generally have an interlocking crystal structure, but no alignment of minerals (Figure 8a and b).

Metamorphic rocks are also crystalline, but here the mineral grains have formed by recrystallization, and replacement of earlier minerals by new minerals, which have grown under the high temperatures and pressures deep in the Earth's crust. Metamorphic rocks often have a 'grain' or directional texture caused by an alignment of minerals, reflecting directed pressure during metamorphism. This is most marked when fine-grained sedimentary rocks, such as mudstones and shales, are changed to slates during metamorphism.

Figure 8 Texture of igneous (a and b) and metamorphic (c) rocks under the microscope: (a) granite—coarse-grained, interlocking crystals of quartz, feldspar and mica; as the magma slowly cooled, individual crystals grew into each other, meeting along very irregular surfaces (the straight line at the bottom is a twin plane within a large feldspar crystal, similar to those in the Shap granite); (b) basalt—fine-grained texture with small 'laths' of colourless feldspar, intergrown with darker patches of pyroxene; the smaller crystal size here indicates much faster cooling than the granite; the Whin Sill has a similar texture; (c) Erquy Red Beds quartzite—compact, interlocking texture, but the outlines of many of the sand grains show that this was originally a coarse-grained sandstone (bottom), grading into medium sandstone (top).

(a)

(b)

(c)

Most igneous and all metamorphic rocks have very low porosity, especially those formed below the Earth's surface at high temperatures and high pressures, where neither water nor air can be trapped between the growing crystals. The interlocking crystalline texture means that both rock types make very tough building stones, good for hostile environments like coastal defences. Most of the high-quality stone used as polished slabs on buildings, and much of the tough wear-resistant aggregate used for roads is either igneous or metamorphic rock.

2.4 Postcard Geological Map

The *Postcard Geological Map** shows the distribution of the main rock groups, and the ages of the sedimentary and metamorphic rocks, for the British Isles. It shows the so-called 'solid geology' — that is, the patterns or 'outcrops' of the main groups of sedimentary, igneous and metamorphic rocks which occur underneath the soil and loose sand, gravel, till, etc.

Activity 3

If you are not familiar with geological maps, you may now like to listen to Audio Band 2, which describes the major sedimentary strata dominating the outcrops of southern England, as a sequence of gently inclined (dipping) layers (beds) towards the south-east. There are much more complicated outcrop patterns in the generally older rocks of highland Britain.

You may find it useful to refer to the rocks and their ages shown on the *Postcard Geological Map* later in the Course, so check your understanding of the map by doing Question 3. (*Note* The red numbers on the map give ages in millions of years, often abbreviated to Ma. These dates differ slightly from the more recent ages in Figure 68, Block 1.)

Audio Band 2   Postcard Geological Map of the British Isles and The Geological Map booklet

Speaker

Dave Williams   The Open University

Question 3

(a)   London and Dublin are both built on rocks shown by a pale brown colour on the map: what is the difference in age between these two strata, and which is more likely to be suitable for use as a building stone?

(b)   Why might the pale green Cretaceous rocks, 65–140 million years (Ma) old, which form the Chalk Downlands, have a westward pointing V-shaped outcrop around London?

(c)   Why is the pale brown stratum that has 'Cardiff' written in it almost surrounded by rocks coloured dark brown?

(d)   A journey in a straight line from London to Edinburgh has been called 'a journey back through time'. How far north do you have to go to reach rocks which are: (i) 200 Ma old;   (ii) 300 Ma old;   (iii) 400 Ma old?
(iv) What can you say about the age of the igneous rocks you meet on this journey?

---

* To be found on the inside cover of the Geological Map booklet.

2.5 Samples in the Rock Kit: describing rocks in hand specimen

It is difficult to appreciate just how variable the solid rocks found in the different parts of the country can be. A selection of rocks, which are typical of widely used building materials discussed in this Block, have been supplied as a simple rock kit. Many of these rocks can be seen on the video bands accompanying this or other Blocks, so that you will get a chance to see the rocks in the field, as well as in the small non-returnable samples in the Kit.

Activity 4

You should now listen to Audio Band 3.

Audio Band 3 Examining the samples in the Rock Kit

Speaker

Dave Williams The Open University

As you listen to the tape, and try to describe and identify the rocks, it would help if you had some means of marking the samples. A good light, preferably daylight, and a magnifying glass would also be helpful. To test for carbonate in the limestones, a few drops of vinegar (acetic acid) will be needed. Use the steel nail in the Rock Kit for scratching the samples.

The main purpose of the tape is for you to be able to confirm for yourself the identification and the properties listed in Table 3.

Colour Easy to recognize, but all rocks vary a good deal in colour, especially where they are exposed to chemical attack by weathering at the Earth's surface, and become stained with brown iron oxides, akin to rust.

Grain size Refer to Figure 7.

Layering Not very useful here, because the samples are all rather too small to show sedimentary layering. The slate has good cleavage planes, along which it splits easily.

Minerals Both the limestones will fizz slowly if put in acids, such as acetic acid (vinegar), giving off bubbles of carbon dioxide. If the rock is a pure limestone, it will eventually completely dissolve in acid.

Pores (porosity) This is a very important property of a rock that is to be used as a construction material. A very porous rock can be shattered if the water held in the pores freezes. A simple test for porosity is to put a drop of water on the sample. If it stays on the surface, the rock is not porous; if it disappears, the rock is porous. If a rock is **permeable**, this means that the pores are interconnected, and so fluids can move through them.

Hardness (estimated by the resistance to being scratched by steel) This is a useful test for separating soft minerals such as calcite from hard ones such as quartz. Limestones can be scratched by steel, but rocks like granite, sandstone and quartzite contain a lot of quartz grains/crystals, which themselves will scratch the steel nail.

Having identified the rock samples, you can then check off their properties in Table 3.

Table 3 Characteristics of the Rock Kit samples

Name	Colour	Crystal or grain size/mm	Layers	Minerals	Pores	Scratched by steel
granite	speckled pink	crystals/2–4 mm (some longer)	no	quartz, feldspar, mica	none	no
basalt	black	crystals/<0.5 mm	no	too small	none	no
Jurassic limestone	buff	grains/0.5–1 mm (rounded)	no	calcite	yes	yes
Carboniferous limestone	dark grey	some grains up to1 mm		calcite	none	yes
Permian sandstone	pink	grains/0.5–1 mm		quartz	yes	no
Ordovician quartzite	grey/pink	crystals up to 1 mm	no	quartz	none	no
Cambrian slate	dark grey	too fine/<0.5 mm	yes	too small	none	yes
Cretaceous flint	brown	glassy	no	too small	none	no

2.6 Stones for building: three examples

Now would be a good time to watch Video Band 4: *Stones for Building* (made in 1993), which illustrates several uses of building stones today, from repair and conservation of old buildings, to the construction of new ones. It illustrates the next three sub-sections of the text, using as examples a sedimentary limestone, a metamorphic quartzite and an igneous granite. After watching the programme, test your under-standing by answering Question 4 (p. 26), which will also serve as a summary of the first part of the programme. It will probably help you to read through this question before viewing the film.

Video Band 4   Stones for Building

Speakers

Dave Williams   The Open University

Julie Berry   narrator

2.6.1   Jurassic limestones

The use of local building stones gives much of the individual character to many parts of this country, as for example is shown for the city of Bath, where most of the buildings since Roman times have been built of the local **oolitic*** limestone. The same Jurassic limestone (in the pale blue on the *Postcard Geological Map* and shown in dark yellow on p. 25 of *The Geological Map* booklet) sweeps north-eastwards through the Cotswolds, up to Yorkshire, and south-westwards to the south coast in the Portland area of Dorset, where there are huge quarries. From here, white, oolitic rock, Portland Stone, has been sent all over the country for well over 100 years. If there is an important civic building near you made of white oolite, it is probably Jurassic limestone, and possibly from Portland (Plate 10, Stockport Town Hall).

This stone has been widely used in Britain's cathedrals, partly because it is fairly soft and so is easy to carve into ornate designs, and also because it is a **freestone**—that is, one that can be cut and split with equal ease in any direction. In other words it is completely homogeneous, and has few natural flaws along which the rock splits preferentially. Porous limestones are easily attacked by acid rain, however, and many old buildings are today slowly being 'eaten' away. The extensive restoration work needed to repair this damage at Winchester cathedral is illustrated, showing that the decay is so bad in some places that the outside 'skin' of the building is having to be replaced piece by piece.

2.6.2   The Erquy Red Beds—changing uses of a 450 Ma quartzite

In Brittany the attractive quartzite of the Erquy Red Beds (ERB) is still being worked in the traditional way by hand, in the quarry and in the mason's yard, to prepare rough blocks of rock for use in houses, flats and shops (Plate 11a). This is very much harder than the oolite, because it is mainly formed of recrystallized quartz grains: it is a metamorphic rock. For over a hundred

---

* The name is based on the egg-shaped particles ('ooids') visible in the Jurassic limestone; a sample is included in the Rock Kit.

years this rock was worked on a huge scale in Erquy (Figure 9a), for making cobbles and kerbstones (Figure 9b and Plate 11b), which were exported by sea, often with onions or cider apples, to ports on both sides of the English Channel, including Brest, Paris, Nantes, St Malo, Plymouth, London, Southampton, Torquay and Cardiff. From South Wales the return cargo was coal (the Brittany coast had no local coal supplies). The distinctive pink and white colour-banded cobbles and kerbs may still be visible in the streets along the English south coast. Today the old ERB quarries are flooded, and are valued as a beauty spot.

Hand dressing of the stone produced spoil heaps of small quartzite chippings, giving a huge tip or scree of waste running down to the sea (Figure 9c). When the first tidal barrage in Europe across the Rance estuary was constructed about 40 years ago, a very large volume of aggregate was needed for concrete in the barrage itself, and the underground turbine hall. The vast heaps of waste quartzite chippings dumped from the quarry to form the screes at Erquy were ideal, since they were only 40 km away. And so today, little of these screes remain at Erquy. In the early 1990s, crushed ERB aggregate was being shipped to Jersey from the Erquy area in 5 000-tonne barges (Plate 26).

The most recent chapter of the ERB story is that in 1991 one of the old quarries was reopened and stone sent to be cut and polished, to produce very attractive slabs of extremely hard and durable stone, which is now being used for cladding buildings, as well as for making tables, stools and kitchen work surfaces.

(a)

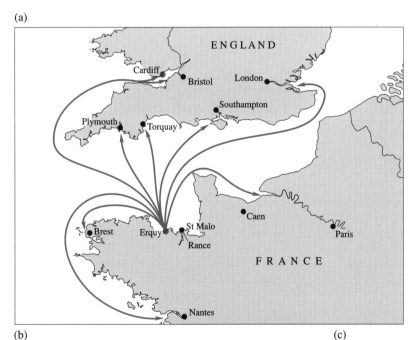

Figure 9 Erquy Red Beds: (a) French and British destinations from Erquy in Brittany; (b) ERB quarries, 1920; gangs of workmen produced squared cobbles and kerbstones for export, which were then lowered down a runway directly into small (100 tonne) ships in the port; (c) screes of waste chippings from the Erquy Red Beds quarries, above the port *c.* 1920.

(b)

(c)

2.6.3 St Malo: an old granite city

St Malo, an important coastal fortress in Brittany for hundreds of years, has been built and rebuilt many times using the local **granite** rocks. In 1944 over half of the buildings of the old city were devastated by Allied action, to flush out German occupiers. However, the thick granite town walls and streets, cobbled largely with Erquy Red Beds, survive more or less intact. The whole city has been rebuilt to the original plan, using the same materials, largely granite, and today it is a tourists' mecca. The tradition of building with the local granite has been applied to several modern structures, such as hotels, and tourist facilities in the old town walls. The almost universal use of the local granite gives a sense of continuity to the architecture, old and new.

Another aspect of the 'granite' tradition can be seen in the port, where large blocks of rock are stacked up on the quay. The international trade in high-quality building stones, mainly granites and metamorphic rocks, brings a wide variety of blocks of rock to St Malo from all over the world, to be cut and polished for use on commercial buildings. An example of these rocks to be seen in St Malo is larvikite (a distinctive blue sparkling igneous rock from Norway), which is widely used in the UK, especially by banks; today many modern buildings are covered with imported rather than UK polished stones.

Using the evidence from Video Band 4, answer the following question.

Question 4

(a)   What evidence was seen in the video to suggest that the ERB were freestones?

(b)   What property of the ERB once made them suitable for cobblestones and kerbstones and now for polished decorative slabs?

(c)   Why were the ERB able to be exported to the UK to be used for cobblestones?

An important general point from the Erquy story is the importance of convenient, especially sea, transport for moving bulk materials: it is unlikely that the huge tips of waste chippings could have been economically moved from distant inland quarries to the Rance barrage.

2.7 Traditional uses of building stones

One of the distinctive features of traditional buildings made in a local style, sometimes called 'vernacular' architecture, is the use of local building materials. Thus, a good guide to the underlying rocks is given by the main material used for these buildings, at least before the railway age. For example, the Jurassic limestone belt (northern part of the blue north-east–south-west belt across England on the *Postcard Geological Map*) is characterized by the use of oolitic limestone (similar to the Jurassic limestone in the Rock Kit), most typically in the Cotswold villages.

A huge area in central England, from Cheshire through Leicestershire to Nottingham and Yorkshire is underlain by the red sandstones of the Permian and Triassic rocks (190–280 Ma), and these are found again around Carlisle (Penrith sandstone). This sandstone, which is included in the Rock Kit, is another freestone, and is widely used for local buildings (see Plate 12).

Other examples of vernacular architecture can be seen in Aberdeen and Cornwall, where for hundreds of years the local granite (red 'blobs' on the *Postcard Geological Map*) was used for many buildings. In south-east England, where hard rocks are scarce, broken **flint** cobbles have traditionally been used for facing buildings (see Plate 13). Nearly all the coloured boxes in the column alongside the *Postcard Geological Map*, representing rocks of all ages, contain rocks that have been used at some time for building.

2.7.1 Costs of building stones

Buildings made from natural stone like oolitic limestone may be aesthetically attractive and durable. However, building in stone today is not cheap, because the cost of dressing the stone to the required size and shape has to be added to that of quarrying, and these processes can never be as mechanized as brick production. Also, however the stones are prepared beforehand, the building process itself is slower, requiring more skill, and so building in stone is always a more costly process than building with bricks.

But what of the cost of producing building stones themselves? Table 4 gives some typical figures for building stone and other building materials.

From Table 4 it is clear that several of the cheapest building materials, such as sands and gravels, can be extracted from the ground for much less than £10 per tonne. Bricks and cement are also quite cheap because the raw materials can be easily extracted, and their processing, though complex, is highly mechanized. However, building stone has to be worked to shape after extraction, and it is these *processing* costs that make natural stone expensive today.

Table 4 Typical early-1990s costs of building materials at the place of extraction

Material	Working methods	Processing	% waste	On site value* (1992 £ t^{-1})
cut and polished stone, as thin slabs	wedging, cutting, low explosives†	diamond saws and polishing	50–90	2 000 (for polished slabs)
large blocks of stone ready for cutting and polishing	wedging, cutting, low explosives	prepared as 3–20 t flaw-free squared blocks	40–90	100–400
slate for roofing	wedging, cutting, low explosives	trimming, hand splitting	80	400–1 500
building stone, dressed blocks	wedging, cutting, low explosives	guillotining, trimming, hand dressing	30–50	50–200
building stone, large blocks	wedging, cutting, low explosives	none, except simple dressing	<10–30	25–100
crushed rock	high explosives	crushing, grading	<10	3–6
sands and gravels	mechanical diggers	sieving, washing	<10	2–5
cement from limestone and shale	mechanical diggers (high explosive)	grinding, mixing, firing, grinding	<10	60–70
gypsum	mechanical diggers	grinding, washing	10	40
bricks and tiles from clay	mechanical diggers	grinding, moulding, firing	<3	50–200

* Prices are given in £ per tonne. Polished stone is usually sold by the square metre (£100 m^{-2}), and bricks are sold per thousand (£100–200).

† Low explosives 'burn', to produce a rapid increase of gas pressure to split the rock apart with minimal shattering. High explosives shatter rocks by producing a shock wave, which travels through the rock at the speed of sound, and so cannot be used for quarrying where dressed or polished stone is being won.

The extreme case of adding value by processing in Table 4 is that of polished granite, where, after quarrying, the rock must first be carefully split into large regular blocks free from cracks, and then cut with diamond saws, and finally polished to give a product that can be worth several *thousand* pounds per tonne.

For many building materials today, there is also a high degree of *substitution* possible, especially for houses. Traditionally, houses in south-east England had all their walls made from bricks, but today cement blocks or timber-and-plasterboard are normally used for most internal walls. Roofing 'slates' can be of naturally split rock (true slate), clay, cement or plastic-based tiles; flat roofs are usually made of concrete, covered with bitumen, lead or copper, a classic case of substitution (Block 1, Section 1.4).

2.8 Transport of building materials and place value

All building materials are heavy and bulky to transport. However, as early as the eleventh century the Normans brought their local limestone from Caen, on the Normandy coast, to be used for the more elaborate carved work in many of their new cathedrals in Britain, presumably because their masons knew that this stone was an excellent freestone. A suitable local stone could always be found for the main bulk of a new English building, but for intricate carved work they used a known reliable material from home. Winchester cathedral, the Tower of London and Windsor castle all contain Caen lime-stone, and the elaborate altar screen in Durham cathedral is Caen stone, though carved in London. It is believed that Caen stone was even imported to Waltham Abbey, only 15 km north of the Thames, in the time of Harold — that is, before the Norman Conquest.

This illustrates an important point: even in 1100AD, when moving heavy materials overland by human and horse power was extremely difficult, it was considered worth transporting a good building stone many hundreds of miles *by sea*. Of course, it is very likely that wool, minerals and coal, and other spoils of conquest, were returned to France by the Normans, and so boats coming 'empty' from Normandy would have to be loaded with something for stability; stone for 'ballast' might as well be good-quality limestone from Caen for ecclesiastical and military buildings in the new colony rather than waste rock. Many French masons came to work the stone, as well as architects, monks and other adventurers, all bringing the benefits of Norman civilization across the Channel.

For hundreds of years, ocean-going vessels carrying commercial cargoes one-way have filled their holds with **'ballast'** for the return journey; supertankers today use water as ballast. Ships carrying solid cargoes often filled their holds with rock as ballast, and so places like Newcastle and south Wales, which for many years exported coal, accumulated piles of 'ballast' rocks from all over the world. In some cases this ballast was crushed and used for roads or railway tracks; the word 'ballast' is still used for hard crushed rock, even when it comes from a local quarry.

Towards the end of the eighteenth century, canals began to provide cheaper transport for bulky building stones, and from the 1830s railways made bulk transport overland much cheaper, leading to much wider availability of building materials. Bath stone, for example, was available at rail depots all over the country.

The railways made great changes to other building materials used in the rapidly expanding industrial cities of the mid-nineteenth century. Roofing slates from north Wales, the Lake District and Cornwall could now be carried cheaply wherever the tracks ran, and local roofing materials such as thatch and poor-quality stone were abandoned.

Exploitation of the Oxford Clay (southern part of the blue Jurassic on the map) for brick-making led to a huge industry, with a ready market in London. This gave a rather uniform look to the Victorian terraces of much of southern England — red brick walls and grey slate roofs — and, because it was a cheaper method of construction, it contributed to the decline of the use of building stone for ordinary houses.

During the late nineteenth and early twentieth centuries, many of the larger towns and cities commissioned new civic buildings, such as market halls, swimming baths, town halls, libraries, etc., and these were often triumphs of the mason's craft. One of the most splendid of these, in the so-called 'wedding cake' style, is Stockport Town Hall (Plate 10), built in 1904–8 mainly of Portland stone, but many exotic Italian marbles were used inside.

Another sign of the coming of the railways is still to be seen in the kerbstones of many cities. With steel-rimmed wheels, the carriages and carts of the time would have rapidly eroded all but the very best cemented sedimentary rocks used for cobblestones and kerbstones. Something much tougher was needed — an igneous or metamorphic rock. For towns along the south coast, for example, Erquy Red Beds rock from Brittany could be imported by sea, and granites from as far afield as Cornwall and Scotland had always been shipped to London. But inland it was the railways that provided cheap transport for dressed stone for the first time.

Unfortunately, most of these cobblestones have been removed or covered up, but the original Victorian city kerbstones still remain in great numbers. These massive lumps of crystalline rock, chosen for their hard-wearing properties, are virtually indestructible, and in many cases over a hundred years of wear has given them a rough polish, which reveals the texture of the rock, best seen when wet. In some cases these rocks can be positively identified and traced to their source. For example, kerbstones and polished shop fronts of Shap granite, which comes from a single quarry in Cumbria, can be seen in cities from Leeds to Bedford, and from Darlington to London (Plate 14a); even the bollards outside St Paul's cathedral are made from Shap granite.

2.8.1 Place value

Transport costs are still a vital component of the costs of cheap building materials today, because the cost of moving the material to where it is needed can soon amount to more than the cost at the quarry gate. Where bulk materials are cheap and readily available from local sources, they tend to be produced from many relatively small quarries, each of which supplies its local area. Such materials are said to have a high **place value**.

The *lower* the value of the material at the quarry gate, the *higher* is its place value.

This reflects the fact that as the material is transported from the quarry the cost of transport can soon become prohibitive. Conversely, a high-value material such as polished granite is said to have a *low* place value, because it can be moved long distance without the transport costs significantly increasing its price. Table 5 gives some indication of the range of costs of transporting bulk materials in and around the UK.

Table 5 Load sizes and transport costs for bulk materials in the early 1990s

Method of transport	Max. load/t	Cost/£ per tonne km*	Comments
lorry	20	0.1	flexible, small frequent loads
rail	3 000	0.04	limited to rail system
barge/small ship	5 000	0.016	for canal or coastal sites only
large ship	35 000	0.002	need deep water and special loading facilities
very large ship	70 000	0.001	as above

* A tonne km is the cost of carrying one tonne for a kilometre ($£\,t^{-1}\,km^{-1}$).

Question 5

(a)   From the costs in Table 5, how far can a full lorry load of the cheapest crushed rock (Table 4) be carried by road before the transport cost exceeds the quarry gate cost?

(b)   How far could the same lorry take a 10-tonne load of the cheapest roofing slates before the transport cost exceeds their on-site value?

Question 5 shows how the delivered price of cheap building materials rises very steeply if they are moved very far from the quarry by road. Under some circumstances rail more than halves the cost of road transport, and in modern ships the costs can be almost 1/100th of the cost per tonne km by road. Of course, this is not the whole story because although it may be possible to site a quarry near a port or railhead, construction sites where the building products are used are all over the country, and so the final stage of delivery usually has to be in 20 tonne lorry loads. The transportation of building materials is considered further in Video Band 5 (see p. 109).

Cement (Section 5) and coal (Block 4) are interesting examples of bulk materials (£60–70 per tonne) that are intermediate in value between crushed rock and dressed slate or polished building stone. Cement and coal have traditionally both had a fairly high place value, and so both were made/worked fairly close to where they were consumed, certainly for inland sites. However, since the early Middle Ages coal has been sent to London from places like Newcastle and South Wales by ship, and in the early 1990s coal imports were much in the news because coal from as far afield as Columbia and Australia was being delivered to UK ports at a cheaper price than much UK-mined coal. Cement was once mainly produced fairly locally, but is now being internationally traded. Big blocks of many popular decorative building stones are shipped in bulk carriers to ports anywhere in the world for local cutting and polishing at a price (£150–£400 per tonne) which is cheap compared with that of the final polished slabs (Table 4).

The importance of these examples is that they show how the fall in transport costs in modern large ships has changed the worldwide pattern of trade in physical resources. Today's bulk carriers are not only used to ship physical resources such as coal, oil and iron ore around the globe, but have also even been used for bulk shipments of wastes for disposal from one continent to another.

2.8.2 Building stones today

There has been a marked change in the use of natural stone in ordinary houses in the last 200 years; most local building stones have been replaced by materials such as bricks which are cheaper and easier to use. Local quarries that had been worked for many years to supply stone for the building of nearby towns and cities have now closed, and in many cases have been filled in. Some of those that are left are producing small amounts of stone, much of it for restoration or repair of old buildings such as cathedrals. In some conservation areas, planning restrictions limit the amount of new building in non-traditional materials. In general, the small number of building stone quarries still in production, and the small scale of their operations, makes them fairly 'environmentally friendly'. These quarries do not use high explosives for blasting — which would shatter the stone — or much heavy machinery, and their small output leads to few traffic complaints. In the future it seems unlikely that the building stone industry will return to anything like its former size, although there is some revival of interest in natural building stone.

In commercial buildings there has also been a considerable substitution of natural stone by modern materials: concrete, steel and glass. Where natural stone is still used on modern buildings, it is usually as a thin 'skin', and the tendency seems to be for architects to specify dramatic-looking imported stone, much of it cut and polished more cheaply in the country of origin than is possible in the UK. The main shopping centre in Milton Keynes was for many years the largest consumer of grey Cornish granite, as cut slabs and kerbs, including walls of polished slabs (Plate 14). There are huge reserves of very good and attractive building stones in most regions of the UK, and should fashions change, and the demand increase, abundant supplies could be produced by reopening quarries, provided they have not been filled with wastes.

2.9 Environmental issues and old building stone quarries

Building stones have often been quarried from a particular bed of good-quality stone, and sometimes such a bed was 'followed' underground, to create shallow mines. This has happened in Bath, where much of the stone has come from mines beneath what is now part of the city, some of which date from Roman times, although most are now abandoned. Some of these old mines are causing an environmental problem today.

The old limestone mines of Bath

In the 1720s, mining of limestone began under what is now the Combe Down area of the city of Bath by Ralph Allen, one of the early stone entrepreneurs, who built his fortune on Bath stone and was immortalized as squire Allworthy in Fielding's *Tom Jones*. Over the next 150 years it has been calculated that about 750 000 m³ of high-quality building stone was extracted.

During Victorian times it was widely used throughout the British Isles: an 1856 catalogue quotes a price of 7½d per cubic foot for Combe Down Bath stone, ex quarry (£0.44 t⁻¹ in today's currency, but allowing ×60 for inflation, not far from today's price in Table 4). It also has prices of four different types of Bath stone delivered in any of four different sizes to over 700 destinations, including four in Scotland and ten in Ireland. The price was doubled by the rail journey to London (1s 2½d), more than trebled by rail to Lancaster (2s 1½d), but only increased to 1s 6d by ship to Glasgow.

The stone as mined was soft and easily worked; it hardened when exposed to the air. The method of working was to leave pillars to support the roof while taking the stone from chambers (or 'rooms') between. The larger the chambers and the smaller the pillars, the more stone that could be taken; in some places this was 85–90%. This was considered to be safe provided the chambers were not too big and enough rock was left as stout pillars to support the roof (Plate 15). When the mines were working, there were no houses above, and the roof cover was 4–8 m thick.

However, today, long after mining has ceased, some of the rock pillars have become much thinner by layers of limestone falling off along natural vertical fractures (joints), probably helped by the vibration of modern traffic. Also, rock tends to spall or flake off the exposed surfaces of the roof, further weakening the structure, and in some places the old mine roofs have now worked their way up to within 2–3 m of the ground surface (Figure 10). Surveys of these mines showed how much land is known to be underlain by old workings, where remedial work may be needed (Figure 11). One suggestion is to fill sections of the mine with a mixture of cement and an inert material such as PFA (pulverized fuel ash, a waste product from coal-fired power stations), but a huge amount of material would be required. Bats — now protected species — also live in the mines, and some parts of the mines are considered to have important archaeological features and so be worth preserving.

In 1992 investigations were carried out, and preliminary estimates of £20–£40 million have been made for the cost of making these stone mines safe.

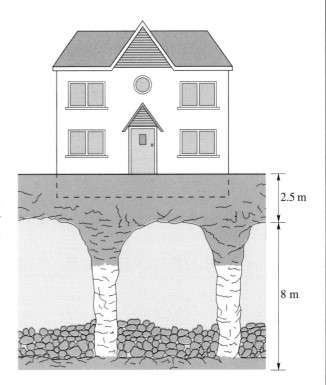

Figure 10 Old limestone mines beneath Bath: the mine roof works upwards with time as flakes of stone fall off both the rock pillars and the roof. The white pillars indicate the limestone bed for which the mine was worked.

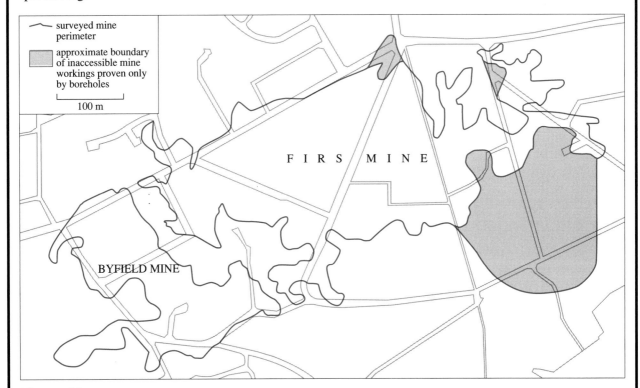

Figure 11 Old limestone mines beneath Bath: map giving rough outline only of mined area. [*IMPORTANT NOTE* The information shown here is not guaranteed, and should not be used for property valuation purposes, etc.]

Question 6

(a) From the information in Figures 10 and 11, what is the approximate total area underlain by the mines, in hectares? (1 hectare = $10\,000\,m^2$ = $1/100\,km^2$)

(b) If the average height of the roof of the mined area is now 2.5 m, how many tonnes of material (sometimes called **grout**) would be needed to fill the mined area shown in Figure 11? Assume that the density of the grout used is $2\,t\,m^{-3}$, and that the pillars do not form a significant volume of the mines.

There are several other cities where old stone mines are found, but if large pillars were left in place, and the rock has not deteriorated, they often form convenient cellars for storage. An example is in Nottingham, where the red sandstone was extensively worked for building stone. (A glimpse of part of one of these can be seen in Video Band 6: *Water for a City*.)

Waste disposal by landfill in old quarries

Many abandoned quarries are in effect themselves valuable 'physical resources'. Today we produce huge quantities of waste, particularly domestic refuse, and the common disposal method is landfill. Old quarries are often seen as the ideal solution to the waste disposal problem and are becoming scarce. If they are filled with waste and then subsequently covered with soil and reseeded, all signs of quarrying can be removed.

But many building stone quarries extracted porous and permeable sedimentary rocks, like sandstones, which may connect to the local water supply. In southern England much of our domestic water supply is pumped from permeable water-bearing strata, called **aquifers**, often from considerable depths (this is discussed more fully in Block 3). Unless old quarries are made water-tight before tipping, wastes are potential sources of contamination of these water supplies. The rate of water percolation through the rocks can be slow, so that by the time contamination is detected it may be many years after the pollution began, and a huge 'plume' of waste may already be contaminating the aquifer (Figure 12). Even if the source of pollution can be immediately identified, it may take years for the pollution to disperse; if the old quarry which is the origin of the pollution has been filled in, grassed over and long forgotten, even locating that source can be a major problem. Since building-stone quarries are generally fairly small, major waste disposal schemes today tend to use the much larger excavations left by other resources, such as brick clays (Section 4).

old sandstone quarry   waste

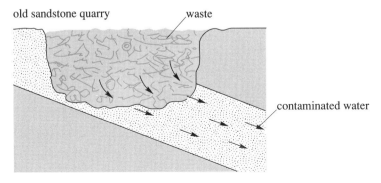

contaminated water

Figure 12 Contamination of an underground aquifer by waste dumped in an old quarry in porous sandstone.

Landscaping and after-uses of old quarries

Some old stone quarries can be made into attractive environmental features, or nature reserves if they are correctly managed, or they can be put to various leisure or educational uses.

Bowlees Country Park — an old quarry as a nature reserve and recreation area

Bowlees Country Park in Teesdale is a disused limestone quarry near a small stream. It is now a nature reserve that is open to the public. Here, Durham County Council has cleared up the remains of old machinery and the piles of quarry waste, allowed the vegetation to regenerate, and developed the area as a nature reserve and public recreational area (Plate 16). The limestone has allowed the distinctive lime-loving flora, including orchids, to prosper in an area where such plants are rare. It also has the advantage that geological features that are not normally visible are here well exposed for study in the stream and the old quarry face by students and members of the public.

Old quarry and mine workings are being developed in this way in several areas of the country as part of the historical and industrial heritage, in some cases helped by the quarrying industry. Perhaps the best example of this is the National Stone Centre at Wirksworth in Derbyshire, where a series of old Carboniferous Limestone quarries have been cleared up and a visitors' centre has been opened. It is possible to discover what the conditions were like here 330 million years ago when the limestone was laid down as a reef in a tropical lagoon, and also to study traditional quarrying operations.

2.10 Summary of Section 2

1 Building materials can all be related to their conditions of formation in different parts of the rock cycle. Features of building stones like grain size and sorting which control how they behave in use, can be related to the geological conditions under which the rocks were formed.

2 The sequence of rocks formed in the UK over the last 1 000 million years can be interpreted from the patterns shown on the *Postcard Geological Map* of the UK (Audio Band 2).

3 Samples of common rocks in the Kit are described on Audio Band 3.

4 The uses of rocks with different physical properties for various building purposes was illustrated in Video Band 4: *Stones for Building*, based in the Bath area and on the north Brittany coast.

5 The importance of cost, and the crucial contribution that transport makes to costs of building materials, is related to the concept of place value. The lower the cost of a material, the higher is its place value.

6 Environmental consequences of building stone extraction include the problems of mine collapse, and groundwater contamination from waste disposal.

3 SANDS AND GRAVELS AS AGGREGATES

3.1 Introduction

Aggregates* can be loosely defined as rock and mineral fragments that can be compacted to a firm mass to fill a space; they are often bound with cement to make concrete, or with bitumen for road surfacing. Although today there is some recycling of crushed bricks and concrete, this accounts for only a tiny proportion of the market; most aggregates are still dug from the ground. Good aggregates are prepared from a mixture of different sizes, chosen so that they can be compacted to give a stable mass with a fairly low porosity.

Huge amounts of unbound aggregates are used below new roads, or to provide flat surfaces below the concrete floors of new buildings; this material is given the general name of **fill** (or 'hard core'), and usually uses whatever materials are readily available and cheapest. Fill must be able to be compacted to provide a stable base, which will not move under the loads to be applied later.

Aggregate sizes

The terms used in the construction industry for different sizes of aggregates are shown in Figure 13, together with the geological terms used in Figure 7 for comparison. 'Sand' and 'gravel' apply to different *sizes* of materials, and there is broad agreement between engineers and geologists about what is called a 'sand'. Also the engineer's **'fines'** (<0.075 mm) are the geologist's 'mud, clay and silt'. **'Fine aggregate'** (0.1–5 mm) is the geologist's 'sand and granules', and **'coarse aggregate'** (5–40 mm) includes most of the geologist's pebbles. If a binding agent such as cement is to be used, aggregates do not

Figure 13 Size fractions of sediments and sedimentary rocks used by geologists (from Figure 7) and engineer's aggregate sizes (below).

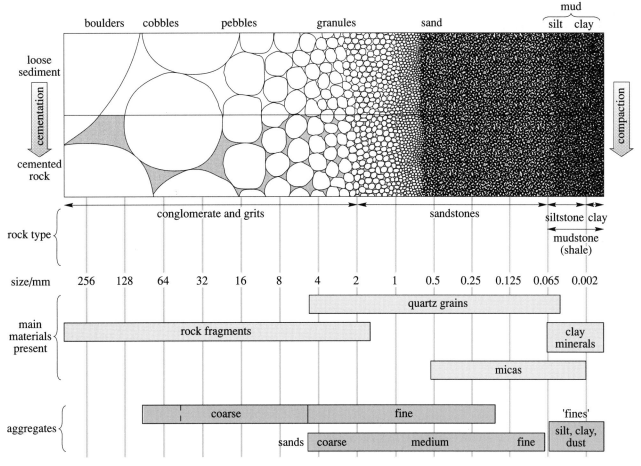

* The term 'aggregate' is the collective word for 'sand', 'gravel' and 'crushed rock'. All of these three materials are 'aggregates'.

usually include material above about 40 mm, but coarse aggregates sometimes use material up to about 75 mm (hence the broken line in the coarse aggregate box in Figure 13). Pebbles coarser than this are either rejected, or have to be crushed before use.

'Fines' (naturally occurring clays and muds) can present a problem for aggregates to be used for concrete or asphalt, because they tend to coat the larger particles and so stop the binding agent getting a good grip. Therefore, 'muddy' aggregates must be washed to keep the fines below 10% (in some cases below 3%) of the total. This means that a sand and gravel deposit that contains a lot of 'fines' is much less desirable than one where the natural processes have carried away all the fine sediment, leaving a resource that can be dug out and used immediately. 'Sands' are largely quartz. Gravel fragments, made of rocks of various sorts, need to have a high crushing strength to make a good aggregate. Gravels containing fragments of weak rock pose real problems for the engineer: the aggregate may crumble under pressure as the rock fragments break.

○ Why do you think that fine grain sizes are not generally used in aggregates used as 'fill' (compare Figures 6b and e)?

○ The 'fines' contain a lot of clay minerals, which under pressure tend to slowly compact as water is lost, making a clay-rich fill, which is liable to shrinkage. This is why holes dug in the road are usually filled with a sand and gravel mixture, which is easily mechanically compacted to a stable mass with firm grain-to-grain contacts (Figure 6b), and so unlikely to settle further.

3.1.1 Growth of aggregate demand in the twentieth century

Aggregates have been used to support railway tracks since the 1830s, where they are still known as ballast (Section 2.8). These days, such aggregates are of crushed rock. But aggregates have only become a really significant building resource in this century, especially with the growth in the use of concrete. Aggregates bound by either cement or bitumen are the main materials used in roads, which today provide the highest single demand for aggregates.

Figure 14 shows that aggregates are largely a twentieth-century phenomenon. It also shows their dramatic rise in production over the last 70 years, as concrete has progressively replaced natural stone and brick for many major construction projects. The 'blips' on the graph are related to slow-downs in economic activity, which always have a dramatic effect on the construction industry.

Important note on 'sorting' of natural sediments and aggregates

1 Engineers describe a good aggregate as a **well-graded material**. For the engineer, a poorly graded aggregate is one with fragments all of the same size, which will form a weak porous aggregate, full of spaces. The term 'sorting' is also sometimes used *in engineering in exactly the opposite sense to the geological one*. For an engineer making concrete, a well-graded or well-sorted material is one that contains a wide variety of grain sizes, and so compacts down to make a strong, dense, low-porosity material. Such a material if found in nature *would be called by a geologist 'poorly sorted'*.

2 'Soil' to an engineer includes any soft material that can be excavated and compacted in a similar way to true topsoil. Sometimes it is also called 'earth', as in earth dams (Block 3).

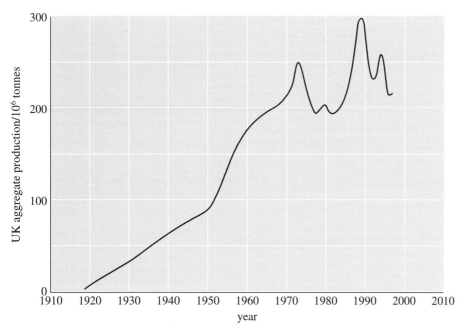

Figure 14 Growth of UK aggregate production in the twentieth century. Very little was produced before 1920, when building stone and brick dominated the building industry.

Today there are three separate sources of aggregates:

(a) Sands and gravels, lying on top of solid rocks at the Earth's surface, which can be regarded as 'natural' aggregates, 'recently' produced by the rock cycle. These consist of loose and uncemented materials which can easily be dug out of shallow workings, and have been the traditional source of aggregate supply in the lowlands of southern England, close to the main population centres and the roads that link them. They are the cheapest because they often only need washing and sieving before use; no expensive crushing is needed. Most sand and gravel deposits are extracted from shallow pits in river valleys, but some submarine resources are also worked (Section 3.4).

(b) Recyclable dumps of waste materials, produced by recent human activities such as mining and steel-making. These can be regarded as the products of a kind of 'human rock cycle'. They account for only a small percentage of aggregates used today, but there are considerable stocks available, and their use is likely to increase in the future (Section 3.6).

(c) Crushed rock or 'hard rock' aggregates, prepared by quarrying solid rocks, and then crushing and sieving the fragments to give the mixture of sizes needed for each particular use.

Before looking at the geological setting of sand and gravel aggregates, first try a couple of simple calculations to put the scale of the aggregates industry in more familiar terms.

Question 7

(a)   What volume of rock has to be quarried to produce 1 million tonnes of material, if there is no waste, and the material being extracted has a density of about 2.5 tonnes per cubic metre ($2.5\,\mathrm{t\,m^{-3}}$)?

(b)   If this 1 million tonnes was extracted in a year from a $50\,\mathrm{m} \times 100\,\mathrm{m}$ quarry (approximately the area of a football pitch), how deep a hole would be created?

Question 8

Imagine that all the aggregates produced in the UK in 1989 came from a single vertical quarry face 20 m high and 50 m wide.

(a)   How many kilometres would this face need to be advanced in a year? (Again assume no waste, and a rock density of 2.5 t m^{-3}.)

(b)   How fast (in metres per hour) would this face be travelling towards your house if it lay directly in the path of the quarry? (Assume 24-hour working, 365 days a year.)

It is clear from these calculations that the volume of raw material removed by the quarrying industry is vast indeed; the sizes and shapes of the holes left in the ground will depend on the type of deposit from which the material is extracted.

Figure 15 shows how the sources of aggregate supply have changed over recent years, with a marked increase in the use of crushed rock in the last 30 years.

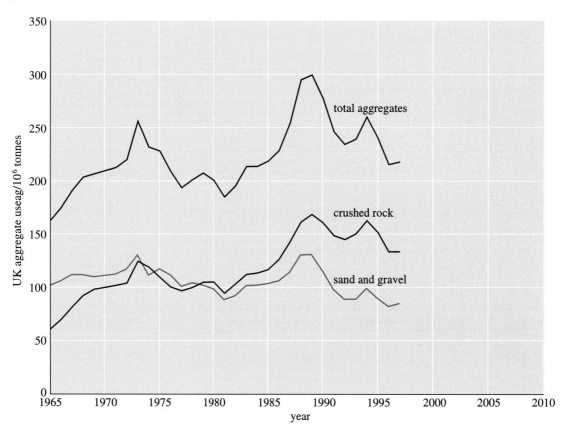

Figure 15   Varying proportions of sands and gravels (natural aggregates), and crushed rock aggregates used in the UK 1960s to 1990s.

Question 9

How has the relative proportion of aggregates between sands and gravels on the one hand, and crushed rock on the other, changed over each of the following 10-year periods: 1965–75, 1975–85 and 1985–95?

Although the data from this graph cannot be used to predict with any certainty what will happen in five years' time, the trend away from sands and gravels to crushed rock aggregates is clear. This trend is not confined to the UK; in

France, sand and gravel dropped from 72% to 53% of the aggregates market between 1970 and 1990. The type of rocks and the quarrying methods involved in the production of crushed rock aggregates are quite different from those used for sands and gravels. We shall look at crushed rock aggregates in Section 7. In this Section we shall start with the geologically simpler sands and gravels. The UK in the early 1990s has over a thousand sand and gravel pits where aggregates are extracted, and many of these are very small scale, serving only a very local area. This reflects the very high place value of sands and gravels, since they are the cheapest of all building materials (Table 4).

3.1.2 Uses of aggregates

But what are aggregates used for? Table 6 gives some typical amounts of aggregate used in different types of construction.

Table 6 Approximate amounts of aggregate for various construction purposes

Construction	Aggregate needed/t
1 m^3 concrete	2
house, 3-bedroom detached	50
multi-storey car park	17 000
15-story office block	50 000
major road	7 500 km^{-1}
new railway line (French TGV)	15 000 km^{-1}
new motorway, or airport runway	100 000 km^{-1}
Channel Tunnel lining	1.5 million

The balance of the use of aggregate will vary from one part of the country to another, and from time to time, as phases of house building, road developments and major construction projects change, but it is possible to break down the overall average uses of aggregate in the UK for a particular year (Table 7).

Table 7 Use of aggregates in the UK in 1991

Aggregate end usage	Aggregate consumption/10^6 t	% of total
roads	78	32
houses	61	25
public works other than roads	39	16
offices, shops	34	14
factories, warehouses	32	13
totals	*244*	*100*

Another way of considering the uses of aggregates would be: one-third roads; one-third houses, offices and shops; one-third industrial and public works. Unless there are major changes in the way we all live, it is difficult to see how the figures in Table 7 are likely to change appreciably. Also, unless there is a policy change — for example, a decision to recycle much more waste material such as old concrete — it is difficult to imagine dramatic changes to the consumption of 'virgin' aggregates shown in Table 6.

An interesting way of comparing consumption between countries is on a per capita basis. For 1988, aggregate consumption in the UK was about 5.2 tonnes per person, Germany 6.7, France 6.8, USA 7.0, Switzerland 8.2,

Denmark 9.0, Finland 10.2, Sweden 10.7, and Austria 11.2. These figures may seem surprising, but because of the wide variation in populations, a large-scale engineering project in a small population country can greatly increase one year's figure. Consider the construction of a new motorway in Belgium, where in 1988 there was a total aggregate consumption of only 36 million tonnes, out of the EU total of almost 2 billion tonnes.

● What would be the percentage increase in per capita consumption if 100 km of motorway was to be built in Belgium in a year?

● 100 km @ 100 000 tonnes per km = 10 million tonnes. In percentage terms, this represents an increase in the total aggregate consumption of

$$\frac{10}{36} \times 100 = 28\%$$

In percentage terms the per capita increase is also 28%.

Here is another example, rather nearer to home.

Question 10

Consider the building of a new housing development for an existing town. There are plans to build the equivalent of 10 000 three-bedroom detached houses (including shops), 12 km of major road, and an 8 km link to the nearest motorway at full motorway standard. How many tonnes of aggregate will be needed?

So even a development to rehouse about 40 000 people requires well over a million tonnes of aggregate, working out at nearly 35 tonnes per person.

3.2 Geology of sands and gravels

3.2.1 Sands and gravels and the rock cycle

Sands and gravels form so-called **superficial deposits,** which are found in all river valleys. They have not been cemented or compacted to any degree, and are known as **unconsolidated deposits**. They occur as generally thin (up to 10 m) irregular layers and 'pockets', lying on top of the 'solid' rocks, and are not shown on the *Postcard Geological Map*. All loose material on top of the solid rock strata is sometimes called by the general term **drift**.

What is the origin of sands and gravels? Weathering and erosion, especially of the exposed rocks in highland Britain, is constantly providing fresh mineral grains (sand) and broken rock fragments (gravel), which are carried to the lowlands by streams and rivers. Occasional severe storms can swell rivers to carry many times their 'normal' load of sediment, but the *rate* of these processes today is much less than during the last glacial period. The present operation of the rock cycle is unable to renew the main sand and gravel deposits that are being worked today at anything like the current rates of extraction. Therefore, although sands and gravels are still being laid down in river valleys today, they are not really a renewable resource.

Similar erosion processes are 'eating away' at the cliffs along much of the coast, to produce the sand and gravel deposits found on beaches. Most of this material will eventually be deposited in the sea; some commercially important supplies of sand and gravel are now taken from the sea (Section 3.4).

The last ice age: Britain in Pleistocene times (Section 3.2.2)

The northern part of the country was several times covered by an ice-sheet, which at one time was hundreds of metres thick at its edge just north of London, and several kilometres thick further north; the ground was permanently frozen (permafrost) almost to Spain. So much water was locked up in ice-sheets that sea-level was 120 m lower than it is today (Figure 16a). This was just one of many cold episodes with very warm periods between: about 120 000 years ago hippopotamuses are known to have roamed as far north as Leeds. Figure 16b shows where many important sand and gravel deposits that have been worked for aggregates are found; many of the largest of these are of glacial or glacifluvial origin.

⬤ It is clear from Figure 16 that many of the sand and gravel deposits worked today are in southern Britain towards the edge of the ice, or outside the ice-sheet. Why do you think this is so?

⬤ There are two distinct reasons. Population density is highest there, so local *demand* for aggregates is highest. Also in areas that were once covered by an ice-sheet, much of the loose material on the surface such as soil, sand and gravel will have been scraped off the solid rock and carried towards the edge of the ice-sheet, to be deposited either directly from the melting ice as unsorted *till* (boulder clay), or as sorted sands and gravels deposited by meltwaters from the ice.

The streams draining off the ice will coalesce to form rivers, and lakes may develop in places, so the sediment will be *sorted* and deposited according to its grain size —*fine* material in *low-energy environments* (clays in glacial lakes), and *coarser* material (sands and gravels) in the *higher-energy environments* of rivers. Most deposition occurred in the summer after each spring thaw.

Each time the climate warmed up and an ice-sheet melted rapidly, all the material still held in the ice itself, from boulders to finely ground 'rock flour', will have been left behind as a *poorly sorted* mass of sediment, to give a covering of till which still 'blankets' large areas of northern Britain today. Because of the wide range of grain sizes, and especially the amount of fines present, till is not an important aggregate resource.

The glacial sands and gravels of southern England, formed beyond the edge of the ice-sheet, have been very widely exploited as aggregates, and many of these have been further transported and sorted ('reworked') by rivers since glacial times to form the sands and gravels found in the valleys of major rivers today. Each time sands and gravels are reworked, sorting improves, since the fines will tend to be carried further. This leaves a generally coarser-grained, better-sorted deposit, which is more valuable as an aggregate. Most of today's commercial sand and gravel deposits, offshore as well as onshore, were probably largely formed by reworking of original glacial material.

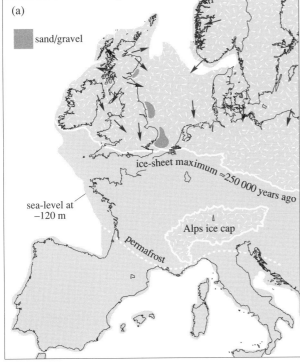

(a)

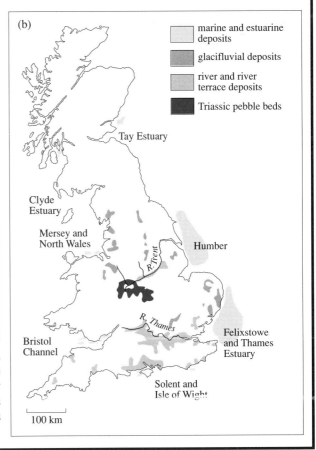

(b)

Figure 16 (a) Maximum extent of the ice caps and frozen ground in northern Europe, about 250 000 years ago, with the sea 120 m below present-day level; the land area is shown by a dark tone; (b) major areas where onland and offshore sands and gravels have been worked in the UK; glacifluvial deposits were formed by streams from melting ice.

Sands and gravels are mixtures of transported rocks and minerals. The finer sand particles are largely mineral fragments, chiefly quartz, whereas rock fragments form the pebbles and cobbles. These materials represent the debris of weathering and erosion, whereby the land surface is gradually being worn away, and all the eroded material is being carried seawards by rivers. Most of the really fine sediment (muds and clays) is carried in suspension to the sea, and is deposited in quiet conditions, such as are found in estuaries or in deeper water out to sea.

 Why are large pebbles of soft rocks rarely found in river gravels?

 The high-energy environment which is needed to transport large pebbles would rapidly break down all softer rocks during transport. Pebbles that survive river transport tend to be of hard crystalline rocks like granites or quartzites, or of well-cemented sediments, chiefly sandstones and limestones.

3.2.2 Glacial sands and gravels

Today, the rivers of the UK carry huge quantities of soil, sand and some rock fragments towards the sea, and over the years much of this material has been deposited in the valleys of large rivers such as the Thames, Severn and Trent. However, present-day conditions cannot explain the large deposits of coarse-grained pebbly material commonly found not only near the rivers themselves, but also as 'sheets' or terraces on the valley sides far above the present rivers.

Most of the important sand and gravel deposits in the UK owe their origin at least in part to conditions in the last glacial period, when both freeze–thaw and the grinding action of moving ice-sheets caused rapid erosion of the land surface in upland areas. It has been estimated that moving ice can erode the rock surface below by as much as 1 mm per year. At the edge of the melting ice-sheets, huge quantities of water were released, together with all the rock and mineral fragments trapped inside the ice. From the edge of the ice-sheet, especially when the climate was warming up, vigorous rivers carried these sediments away to spread sheets of sands and gravels along the valleys of Britain, and over land that is now part of our surrounding sea. When the last ice melted and sea-level reached present-day levels, these became offshore deposits (Section 3.4).

3.3 Aggregates from river terrace sands and gravels

Present-day **river terrace deposits** tend to occur as more or less irregular strips of sand and gravel, at definite heights along the sides of major river valleys, corresponding to the various levels of the flood plain of the river in past times. The oldest terraces are the highest; the youngest occupy the present flood plain of the river. A typical section across the Thames in central London is shown in Figure 17. Two older terraces are evident, as well as deposits of the present flood plain. Workable sands and gravels can be found in all these terraces, but gravel pits in the older, higher, terraces are less liable to flooding when the aggregate has been extracted. Clearly, any materials taken from below the present river level must lie below the **water table** (the level in the ground below which the rocks are saturated with water), and so any excavations here will fill with water.

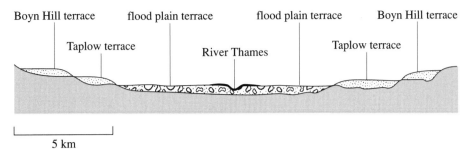

5 km

Figure 17 River valley terrace deposits in the Thames valley. The oldest deposits are on the top terraces; each lower terrace marks a later stage when erosion of the river had cut the valley deeper. The most recent gravels are those on the flood plain at the bottom of the valley.

Terrace and flood-plain deposits provide good-quality aggregates, because the rivers that deposited them have carried away most of the useless 'fines'. It is fortunate that many of our large urban areas are in major river valleys containing large deposits of sand and gravel; the best example is the Thames and its tributaries around London. In fact some of the best river terrace deposits lie in the Heathrow area, and although some of these have been worked, and can be seen as lakes today, huge reserves of sand and gravel have been covered up ('sterilized') by the building of the airport (Figure 18).

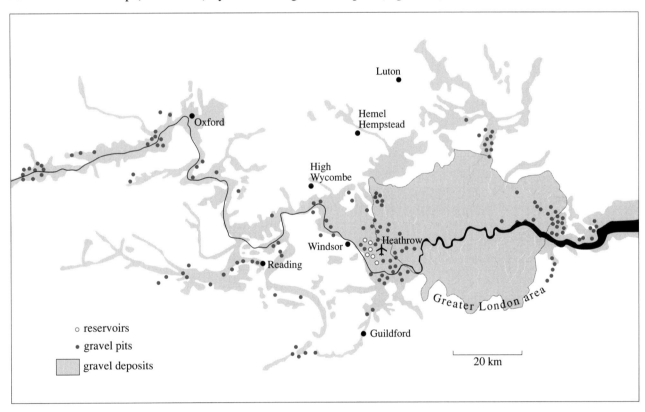

Around Oxford, most of the pebbles in the river gravels are of Jurassic limestone (blue on the *Postcard Geological Map*) similar to the Bath stone sample in the Rock Kit, but nearer to London the gravels are mainly of flint. The sample of flint in the Kit came from such a gravel. The main flint-containing rock to the north of the London basin is the Chalk (green on the *Postcard Geological Map*), and so this must be the source of these gravels.

Figure 18 Gravel deposits in and around London. The Thames and most of its major tributaries have workable sand and gravel deposits.

Question 11

In the Chalk exposed in a road cutting, flint accounts for less than 10% of the total rock. How would you explain why the pebbles in the river gravels near London contain very few Chalk pebbles?

Aggregates from river terrace deposits are dug out of open pits by mechanical diggers, and sorted into the different sizes by sieving. Stockpiles of the different sizes are then kept for dispatch, eventually to be blended for the particular mix of sizes required. The only processing needed is washing to remove fines, and screening out of any large pebbles.

There is always some **overburden** of topsoil, subsoil or river mud and silt, which is too fine-grained for processing, and so has to be stripped off the top of the gravel. Today, overburden is stored in **bunds**, linear banks which act as screens to the works and which are often used to restore the site after extraction.

For a deposit to be economic the overburden should not be more than about a metre thick, and also should not be more than about a third of the thickness of the sand and gravel deposit being worked. This is often expressed as a ratio: for low-value materials like sands and gravels, the **overburden ratio** (overburden : workable deposit thickness) should be less than 1 : 3. In other words, there should be at least three times more extractable gravel than overburden present.

You will find in later parts of the Course that for higher-value resources such as limestone (Section 5, this Block) or open-cast coal (Block 4), which are also extracted from open pits, the overburden ratio can be much higher than this: overburden ratios of 5 : 1 to 20 : 1 are not uncommon these days for more-valuable materials.

Like all sedimentary materials, sands and gravels tend to occur in layers. Sedimentary deposits laid down in the sea are often in even layers that can be of almost constant thickness over many hundreds of square kilometres, reflecting the uniform conditions of deposition in the ocean. However, conditions were very different in the streams and rivers that laid down river gravels. Conditions of deposition can change rapidly and frequently with variations in season and climate, and an individual deposit was often confined to a single valley. This means that most sand and gravel deposits are small and very variable: they generally occur in more-or-less lens-shaped bodies along the sides and the bottom of river valleys. These 'lenses' generally are between a few hundreds of metres to a few kilometres in length, tens of metres wide, and a few metres thick.

Deciding how much material is present in a sand and gravel deposit, and whether it is an economic prospect to develop or not, requires a detailed knowledge of the size and composition of the deposit before work begins. The normal method is to drill a pattern of holes, from which the thickness of both the overburden and the deposit can be worked out, and to take samples for particle size analysis by sieving.

Consider the information given in Figure 19 and Table 8, and then try to answer the following question.

Question 12

(a) How much further is it worth extending the gravel workings in Figure 19, assuming it is only economic to work with an overburden : gravel ratio of less than 1 : 3? Complete rows c to e in Table 8.

(b) How many tonnes are there to be worked within this ratio? (Assume that the gravels have a density of 2 t m^{-3}.) Complete the bottom row in Table 8.

Exploration of a sand and gravel deposit

Figure 19 shows how exploration can be carried out to see how far an existing gravel pit can be worked economically. From a grid of boreholes (A–H) drilled at one end of the gravel pit, the thicknesses of overburden and gravels can be measured, and hence the volume, and so tonnage, of extractable gravels present can be determined. Below the gravels lies a bed of clay. The thicknesses of overburden and gravels are given in Table 8. If each borehole is taken to be representative of the 10 m × 10 m block in which it is centred, it is possible to work out whether it is worth extending the workings, and how much gravel can be extracted economically. Plate 17a shows a working gravel pit; Plate 17b is a close-up view of a typical Thames valley flinty gravel.

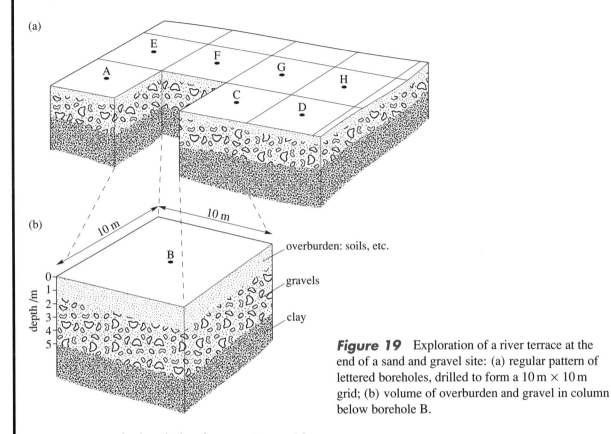

(a)

(b)

overburden: soils, etc.

gravels

clay

depth /m

Figure 19 Exploration of a river terrace at the end of a sand and gravel site: (a) regular pattern of lettered boreholes, drilled to form a 10 m × 10 m grid; (b) volume of overburden and gravel in column below borehole B.

Table 8 Logs for boreholes shown in Figure 19

Depths in boreholes/m	A	B	C	D	E	F	G	H
(a) to top of gravels	1.0	1.5	1.0	1.5	0.5	1.0	2.0	1.0
(b) to bottom of gravels	4.5	5.0	5.0	2.5	1.5	2.5	3.0	3.5
(c) thickness of gravels/m (b − a)								
(d) overburden ratio (a : c)								
(e) economic? (yes or no)								
(f) tonnes of gravel in 10 m × 10 m column (= c × 10 × 10 × 2)								

There are more sophisticated methods of plotting the thicknesses of masses of rock and ore bodies in the ground, by preparing maps that contour either the top or bottom surfaces (or both) of the material being assessed, and even by preparing maps contoured to show the thickness of the resource. But these are more often used when the resources are of higher value than sands and gravels.

3.4 Offshore sand and gravel deposits

In glacial periods when sea-level was very much lower than it is today (Figure 16a), much of the North Sea would have been above sea-level, and beneath the ice for much of the time. During major melting of that ice, powerful rivers all around the edges of the ice cap would have carried sheets of sand and gravel across the surrounding land surface including what is now the North Sea. Once covered by the sea, the action of currents and tides would tend to winnow out the finer sediment to leave well-sorted sands and gravels, well suited to aggregate production. Several of these glacial sheets of sand and gravel are now being exploited around our coasts by submarine dredging (Figure 16b). A typical dredger 'hoovering up' aggregate is shown in Figure 20. Aggregates from the sea must be well washed to remove salt, especially if they are for use in concrete.

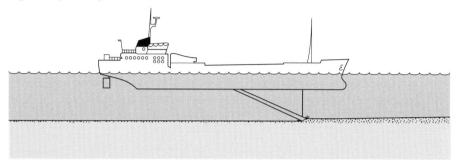

Figure 20 Dredger sucking up sands and gravels from the bed of the North Sea.

Up until the 1960s less than 3 million tonnes of sand and gravel a year were produced from the sea around Britain, but this rose to almost 20 million tonnes by the early 1990s, approaching 20% of the total sand and gravel output of the UK. However, in the longer term it is likely that concerns about the possible effects of exploitation of these deposits on marine life on the one hand, and on coastal erosion due to the extraction of huge tonnages of sea-floor sediment on the other, will limit the growth of this industry.

Fossil desert dune sands in Durham and beneath the North Sea

In Durham, a bed of uncemented sand is widely exploited for building sand. It is about 280 million years old and was laid down in a Permian desert (Permian rocks are shown as a thin north–south orange strip on the *Postcard Geological Map*). The sands are of very well-rounded quartz grains of uniform grain size (0.5–1 mm diameter), and are ready for use in the building industry after a simple screening to remove any larger nodules.

⬤ Since these sands were laid down in a desert, would you expect them to be well or poorly sorted, and of high or low porosity?

◯ Desert dune sands are usually well sorted (the wind blows the fine material away), so all the grains left are of similar size. This sand will have a high porosity (Figures 4 and 6a, and Activity 1).

These sands lie immediately above the Coal Measures (upper beds of the Carboniferous, pale brown on the *Postcard Geological Map*) over much of the Durham coalfield. They were infamous in the last century because they were often the cause of accidents when shafts were sunk through them to get at the coal beneath. The sands were full of water and were uncemented. When a shaft reached them, they just 'flowed' into the shaft bottom, as a sand–water slurry.

In the quarries where they are worked in Durham these sands occur just below a well-cemented lime-stone, which is also worked as an aggregate. This provides a good example of a single quarry exploiting two quite different building materials (Plate 18).

These sands are the same age as the red sandstone sample in the Rock Kit, but it has a quartz cement holding the grains together. This makes it a good building stone (Figure 6d; Plate 12), but even so the rock still has a high porosity. This is the same rock formation that is a vital reservoir for much of the gas found under the southern North Sea (Block 4).

3.5   Old sand and gravel deposits

Some deposits of sand and gravel are much older than the geologically recent materials discussed in the preceding Sections, but have remained more or less uncemented for hundreds of millions of years, and so can still be easily worked in the same way as superficial deposits. Examples are the sandy pebble beds of the Midlands, of Triassic age, about 200 million years old (visible along the M6, just north of Keele; see also Figure 16b), and the sands of Cretaceous age (100 million years old), which are commonly worked in south-eastern England. (See also Permian sands box opposite.)

3.6   Aggregates from wastes

Over 3 billion tonnes of industrial waste has accumulated during the past two centuries in the UK: most of this is in spoil heaps from coal mining, but tips from roofing slate quarries, sand from china clay production and ash from power stations are also important, and some of these can be used as a substitute for sands and gravels. Table 9 shows the size and locations of the accumulated stockpiles of the more important sources of industrial waste, and the rates at which they are being produced and used in the early 1990s.

With the exception of iron-making slags, where some old stockpiled material is being used in roads, the rest of these materials are still being generated faster than they are being re-used. At the moment it is almost always cheaper to quarry new building materials than to use these wastes.

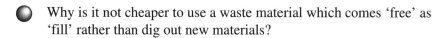 Why is it not cheaper to use a waste material which comes 'free' as 'fill' rather than dig out new materials?

Many of these materials are too remote from potential building sites to make transportation worth while. For example, china clay waste (mainly sand) is only available in the far south-west. In other words, most of these materials have a very high place value.

Table 9   Industrial waste materials, and their uses in the early 1990s (weights in 10^6 tonnes)

Waste	Where found	Stockpile	Annual production	Annual use	Main uses
waste slate	North Wales, Cornwall, Lake District	400–500	2	<1	fill, road foundations
colliery shale*	coalfields	2 000	45	8	fill
pulverized fuel ash (PFA), furnace bottom ash (FBA)†	coal-fired power stations	150–200	13	5	blocks, fill, cement substitute
iron, and steel slags‡	industrial areas	30	6	7	aggregate
china clay sand	Cornwall, Devon	600	27	1.5	blocks, fill, aggregate
old building rubble		0	24	11	fill, aggregate
totals		*3 300*	*117*	*33*	

* Much colliery waste has been left as conical hills, now grassed over, and is unlikely ever to be used. Burnt 'red' shale is best; unburnt 'black' shale can ignite spontaneously due to its sulphide and carbon content, and is too soft for many purposes. The production figure is in rapid decline as more coal is imported.

† FBA is used as a lightweight aggregate because it contains a lot of small 'glass' spheres, which give it good thermal insulation properties. PFA (which collects in power station chimneys) is **pozzolanic**; that is, it sets hard with water, and so can be used as a cement substitute, in blocks or as a grout for filling cavities, such as old mines.

‡ Used mainly for road-building aggregate. Some of the old stockpiles are being used, but others are unlikely to be used because they are in remote locations (e.g. Barrow).

As pressure for all resources to be used in a more sustainable manner increases, and environmental concerns grow, it is likely that re-use of some of these materials will increase.

3.7 Sand and gravel workings — planning and the environment

Many of the best deposits of superficial sands and gravels lie in the lower reaches of the main rivers of lowland Britain, the very places where population pressure puts most demand on the land for building, agricultural or amenity use. Consequently, there are many good sand and gravel deposits which cannot be worked for several reasons. For instance, Heathrow airport has been built on top of a huge deposit of sand and gravel, and it has been calculated that in the London area alone as much as 1 billion tonnes of sand and gravel have been 'sterilized' under built-up areas. When new urban developments are being planned, extracting sands and gravels *before* building begins, or leaving the best sites for future exploitation is clearly the preferred course of action.

Sand and gravel workings in Northamptonshire

The traditional area for supplying most of the sand and gravel required for Northamptonshire has been from the valley of the river Nene, which runs close to the major towns of Daventry, Northampton and Wellingborough, where aggregate demand is highest.

However, by 1990 there were already extensive flooded old workings along the Nene valley, and further permissions for extraction outstanding, and so it was decided to discourage further new workings (Figure 21). Further, a management plan for the whole valley was drawn up, involving restoration of the old flooded gravel pits, and their use for designated purposes in different parts of the valley: fishing, wildlife areas, watersports, etc. Therefore, the county council commissioned investigations to look for alternative supplies of aggregates outside the Nene valley to meet demand in the late 1990s, in the 'sand and gravel area of search' on Figure 21a.

 Why do you think the new sites are to be sought away from the valley floors?

 Because the workings will not flood when extraction is completed, and so the ground can be restored to some other use.

Table 10 shows the results of two trial borings at opposite ends of this area of search, both of which found sand and gravel. Consider these results and then attempt Question 13.

Table 10 Results of two trial borings in 'area of search'*

Log of boreholes	Trial boring A	Trial boring B
height of ground above sea-level/m	160	120
water-table/m	none found	7
topsoil/m	0–0.3	0–0.2
boulder clay/m	0.3–4.4	0.2–0.6
glacial sand and gravel/m	4.4–7.4	0.6–7.4
solid rock/m	7.4	7.4
average sand and gravel composition:		
fines (<0.06 mm)	31%	16%
sand (0.06–4 mm)	46%	49%
gravel (4–64 mm)	23%	35%
sand and gravel thickness/m		
overburden : sand and gravel ratio		

* Depths in boreholes are given in metres below ground surface.

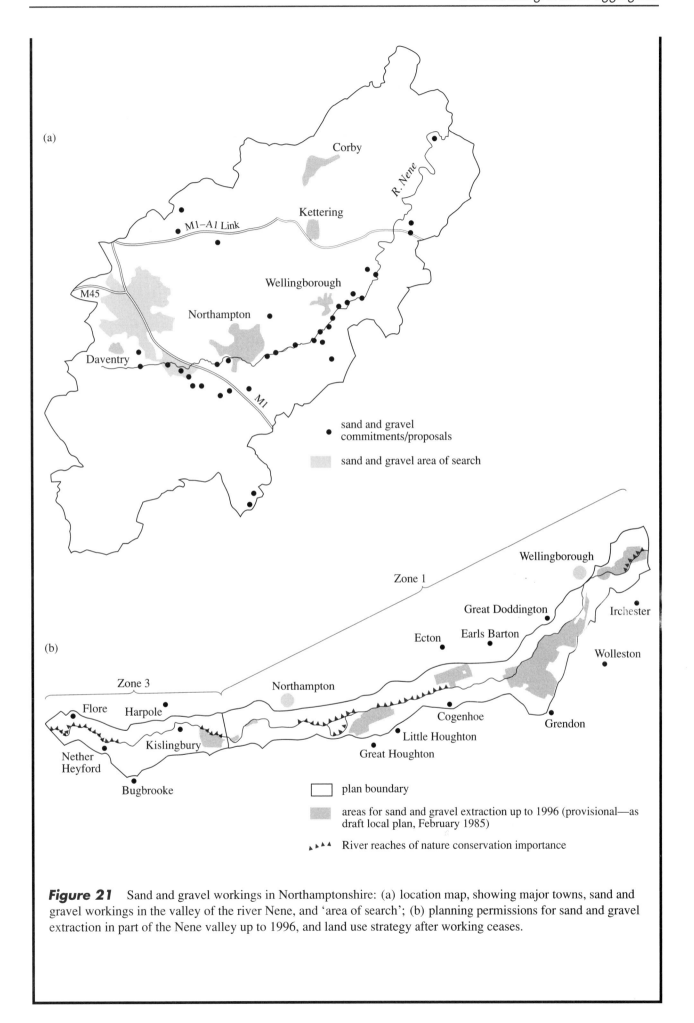

Figure 21 Sand and gravel workings in Northamptonshire: (a) location map, showing major towns, sand and gravel workings in the valley of the river Nene, and 'area of search'; (b) planning permissions for sand and agravel extraction in part of the Nene valley up to 1996, and land use strategy after working ceases.

Question 13

(a)   Complete Table 10 (bottom two rows) in box on p. 48.

(b)   Which deposit looks more promising as far as the overburden ratio is concerned?

(c)   Which deposit looks more promising in terms of the composition of the sand and gravel itself?

(d)   Do you foresee any other problems with either location?

Where sands and gravels are taken from the flood plain of a river, old pits will fill with water to form lakes. In many cases these lakes have been used afterwards as wildlife sanctuaries or for fishing or watersports as a part of the restoration programme. An example of this is the Lower Farm Pit near Newbury (Plate 19).

Dry gravel pits, such as many river terrace sites, can be restored to agricultural use by returning the soil, and landscaping. In some cases, dry sites leave a hole that can be used for tipping wastes, provided that care is taken to prevent contamination of the groundwater if the ground below is permeable.

As the demand for aggregates rose dramatically in the 1980s, there were fears that a crisis of aggregate supply was developing in south-east England, because the rate of sand and gravel extraction was much faster than the rate at which new planning permissions were being granted for future gravel workings. Reserves which have been proved and found to be economic, and which aggregate firms have planning permission to extract, are often called the **land bank**. Traditionally 10-year land banks have been the aim, so that both local planners and the extractive industry could make long-term plans, but in the early 1990s it was suggested that these land banks could be safely reduced to 5 years. This was at a time when there was an increase in the rate at which marine sands and gravels were being developed, and also a rapid increase in the 'importation' of crushed hard rock aggregates into south-east England from more remote quarries. We shall return to this important topic in Sections 7 and 8.

3.8   Summary of Section 3

1   There has been a rapidly rising demand for aggregates this century; the current annual consumption in the UK of about 5 tonnes per capita is towards the lower end of the range for industrialized countries.

2   'Natural aggregates' — sands and gravels — have been the traditional materials used for aggregates.

3   There are large stockpiles of waste material potentially useful for building, and several industries are still generating wastes much faster than they are being used in the building industry. Much more re-use of this material may be possible in the future.

4   In some heavily populated areas, where sands and gravels have traditionally met the local aggregate demand, planning permission for future extraction is becoming more difficult to obtain, casting doubt on the sustainability of this supply.

5   Higher public awareness of environmental issues makes the provision of adequate aggregate reserves for the future an increasing problem.

4 CLAYS AND BRICKS

All natural clays can absorb water, be moulded to shape when wet, and then heated in a kiln (fired) to become hard and strong, like other rocks. All clays used for brick-making contain a high proportion of clay minerals. Clay *minerals* are an essential component of good soils, whereas so-called 'heavy clay' soils are formed by weathering of rocks which themselves are already rich in clay minerals. Geologically, clays may be superficial deposits, laid down since recent glacial times like sands and gravels, or beds of clay rocks up to hundreds of millions of years old, which have been compressed to form mudstones or shales.

The craft of making useful things from clays, like cooking pots and bricks, stretches back to the beginnings of civilization. Porcelain, china and many other ceramics are made largely from clay minerals. The most important building materials made from clays are bricks, but clay has traditionally also been used to make roof tiles, and also 'clay' or 'earthenware' drainage pipes to go in the ground.

4.1 Clays and clay minerals

The properties of clay (rocks) are very variable, but are largely controlled by the particular clay minerals they contain. The chemistry of clay minerals is not simple: there are three main groups of clay minerals, each with distinct properties. Clay rocks usually contain a mixture of clay minerals, giving a wide variety of clays with different properties, and so many different uses. We shall concentrate here on clays used for making bricks, which represent by far the most abundant use of clays.

What do we mean by clay, and clay mineral? At its simplest, a pure clay (rock) is one made up of clay minerals. You have already met the term 'clay' in Figures 6 and 7, where it referred to the smallest sedimentary particles (less than 0.002 mm). If you shake up some soil with water and then let it settle for a few minutes, the finest material, still in suspension and making the water cloudy, will be chiefly small flakes of clay minerals. Most of the finest-grained sediment carried along in running water, and giving it a muddy look, is also mainly clay minerals. The particles are much too small (few thousandths of a millimetre) to be seen with even the highest power (light) microscope (Figure 22).

Figure 22 Clay minerals in clays and mullite needles in bricks: (a) typical six-sided flat flake-like crystals of the clay mineral, kaolinite, photographed with an electron microscope; (b) 'needle'-shaped mullite crystals, formed by heating kaolinite to high temperature during brick-making.

(a)

(b)

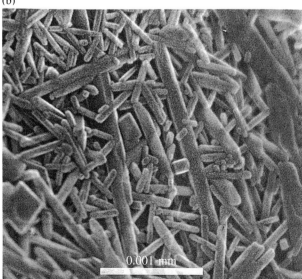

Section 3 was concerned with the *physical breakdown* of existing rocks, by frost, erosion, running water, waves, etc., to produce both rock and mineral fragments, which can be transported and laid down elsewhere as sands and gravels. The minerals found in sands and gravels are essentially those present in the original rocks which are resistant to the processes of weathering and erosion.

So, how are clay minerals formed? They come from the *chemical breakdown* of minerals, at the Earth's surface, chiefly by rainwater, which even in unpolluted areas is slightly acidic due to dissolved carbon dioxide.

What happens when a granite suffers weathering and chemical attack in a wet temperate climate like that in the UK today (Figure 23)? Granite consists mainly of three minerals: quartz, feldspar and mica. The quartz is resistant to chemical attack, and so will be carried away as mineral grains, together with fragments of the original rock, to form sands and gravels along the river valleys. The feldspars and micas, however, are chemically attacked by the action of rainwater to form new (clay) minerals; some of their original elements, especially the sodium, potassium and calcium, are carried away in solution as ions (Na^+, K^+, Ca^{2+}). These clay minerals therefore retain most of the original aluminium and silicon from the feldspar and micas, but contain less of the more soluble ions (Na^+, K^+, Ca^{2+}), which eventually reach the sea.

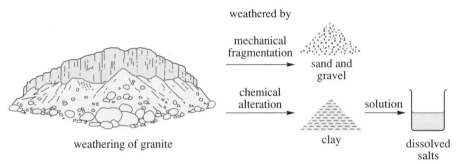

weathering of granite

Figure 23 The weathering of a granite. Physical weathering (such as frost action) splits the rock into fragments, and breaks off resistant quartz grains; these are carried away to form sand and gravel deposits. Chemical weathering attacks the feldspars and micas, which are chemically altered to clay minerals. Very soluble ions (Na^+, K^+, Ca^{2+}) are carried away in solution.

Clay minerals usually belong to one of three main groups: **kaolinite**, **illite** and **montmorillonite**. Figure 24 shows the layer structure of the different clay mineral groups. The layers in kaolinite are held together by fairly weak bonds, but the presence of positively charged metal ions between the negatively charged clay mineral layers in illite and monmorillonite leads to strong bonding between the layers.

Consider what happens in the simplest case, the chemical breakdown of potassium feldspar during weathering to form kaolinite. (Potassium feldspar forms the large pink crystals that you can see in the granite in the Rock Kit.) Feldspars are important as the most abundant minerals in igneous rocks. Unlike pure water, which is neutral, rainwater is acidic because carbon dioxide in the atmosphere dissolves in it before it reaches the ground. Some of the carbon dioxide also reacts with the water to form hydrogen ions and bicarbonate ions (it is the concentration of hydrogen ions which determines the acidity of a solution):

$$CO_2 + H_2O = H^+ + HCO_3^- \qquad (4.1)$$

The overall breakdown of potassium feldspar to kaolinite during chemical weathering can be shown as:

$$2KAlSi_3O_8 + 2H^+ + H_2O = Al_2Si_2O_5(OH)_4 + 2K^+ + 4SiO_2 \qquad (4.2)$$

potassium feldspar   acid rainwater   kaolinite   ions and silica removed in solution

Water combines with the aluminium and some silica of the original feldspar to form kaolinite, while all the potassium and the rest of the silica are carried away in solution, along with the bicarbonate ions derived from the dissolved

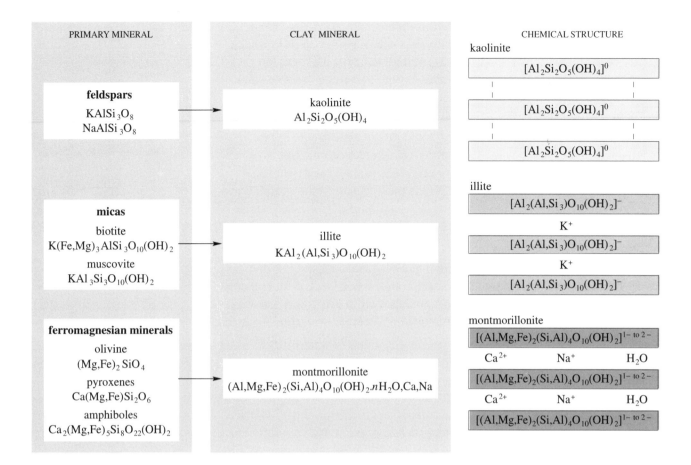

PRIMARY MINERAL

feldspars
$KAlSi_3O_8$
$NaAlSi_3O_8$

micas
biotite
$K(Fe,Mg)_3AlSi_3O_{10}(OH)_2$
muscovite
$KAl_3Si_3O_{10}(OH)_2$

ferromagnesian minerals
olivine
$(Mg,Fe)_2SiO_4$
pyroxenes
$Ca(Mg,Fe)Si_2O_6$
amphiboles
$Ca_2(Mg,Fe)_5Si_8O_{22}(OH)_2$

CLAY MINERAL

kaolinite
$Al_2Si_2O_5(OH)_4$

illite
$KAl_2(Al,Si_3)O_{10}(OH)_2$

montmorillonite
$(Al,Mg,Fe)_2(Si,Al)_4O_{10}(OH)_2 \cdot nH_2O,Ca,Na$

CHEMICAL STRUCTURE
kaolinite

$[Al_2Si_2O_5(OH)_4]^0$

$[Al_2Si_2O_5(OH)_4]^0$

$[Al_2Si_2O_5(OH)_4]^0$

illite

$[Al_2(Al,Si_3)O_{10}(OH)_2]^-$
K^+
$[Al_2(Al,Si_3)O_{10}(OH)_2]^-$
K^+
$[Al_2(Al,Si_3)O_{10}(OH)_2]^-$

montmorillonite

$[(Al,Mg,Fe)_2(Si,Al)_4O_{10}(OH)_2]^{1- \text{ to } 2-}$
Ca^{2+} Na^+ H_2O
$[(Al,Mg,Fe)_2(Si,Al)_4O_{10}(OH)_2]^{1- \text{ to } 2-}$
Ca^{2+} Na^+ H_2O
$[(Al,Mg,Fe)_2(Si,Al)_4O_{10}(OH)_2]^{1- \text{ to } 2-}$

carbon dioxide. As the feldspar decomposes to kaolinite, a tough granite eventually just crumbles away to leave a mixture of unaltered quartz crystals, and a soft mass of the new clay mineral, kaolinite. This process is seen working today most dramatically in wet tropical climates like Brazil, where in a road cutting through hard granite, little fresh rock will be visible within 10–20 years; in the cooler temperatures of the UK, however, weathering reactions tend to occur at a much slower rate. In both environments, acids produced by plants and animals are probably more important than that derived from carbon dioxide. The same kind of reaction is responsible for the attack of granite building stones, like the aqueduct at Segovia (Figure 2). Weathering is greatly accelerated today in industrial areas by sulphur dioxide produced by the burning of sulphur-rich fuels and nitrogen oxides from car exhausts, both of which dissolve in rainwater and increase its acidity.

Generally, micas weather to give illite, which retains some potassium in its crystal lattice, and the ferromagnesian igneous minerals, such as pyroxenes and amphiboles, weather to yield the clay mineral montmorillonite, whose crystal structure contains sodium, calcium and some water (Figure 24).

The important feature shown in Figure 24 is the difference in the ions and molecules *between* the aluminosilicate layers of the three main groups of clay minerals.

Kaolinite   The aluminosilicate layers are electrically neutral, so no ions are needed between the layers to achieve overall electrical neutrality.

Illite   The aluminosilicate layers are negatively charged; overall neutrality is achieved by potassium ions, K^+, between the layers.

Montmorillonite   Here the aluminosilicate layers are more strongly negatively charged; neutrality is achieved by the presence of both calcium and sodium ions between the layers. Note that some water molecules are associated with the positive ions here.

Figure 24 Formation, composition and structure of clay minerals — the relationship between the major groups of original minerals on the left and the composition of the clay minerals that each forms on weathering (centre). The sketches of the structures of the three main clay mineral types (right) show how the negative charges on the aluminosilicate layers of illite and montmorillonite are balanced by the positive charges on metal ions.

The positive ions between the aluminosilicate layers of clay minerals are only loosely bound, and so can be relatively easily replaced by other ions of similar size and charge, which makes some clay minerals useful in ion substitution or 'ion exchange' reactions, a feature sometimes used in water purification. Montmorillonite can also swell up by absorbing huge amounts of water into its layered structure, giving it many useful properties (Section 4.6).

So much for the chemical processes of clay mineral formation, but *where* are clay rocks formed? The simplest type is the so-called **residual clay**, which has not been removed by erosion: the most valuable clay resource of this type in the UK is the china clay (largely kaolinite) of Cornwall, which is today worked from the 'pockets' where it formed by the weathering and alteration of the underlying granite (see Section 4.6.2).

However, clay is a soft and easily eroded material, and so it is easily picked up by running water and carried into streams and rivers. Once in suspension, minute flakes of clay minerals will only be deposited when the river reaches a very low-energy environment such as a lake, estuary or the sea.

Clay minerals tend to carry a small negative charge on their surface. As like charges repel, aggregation of clay mineral particles to larger flakes, which would sink more rapidly, is inhibited in fresh water. Materials that behave in this way are known as **colloids**, and are described as being in **colloidal solution**. Particles in colloidal solution have diameters in the range 10^{-9}–10^{-6} m; in effect, it is a state somewhere between ions in solution and true particles in suspension (that is, those which can be filtered). Colloids are important in the transport of materials to form metal deposits (Block 5 *Metals 1*). When they reach the sea, however, there is a much higher concentration of dissolved positive ions, such as Na^+, K^+, Ca^{2+}, which neutralize the negative charges on the clay mineral surface, and so enable the particles to stick together, a process called **flocculation**. These larger particles then fall to the sea floor to form a layer of sediment. Clays that have been transported and then laid down as sediments are called **sedimentary clays**; these are not usually composed of a single clay mineral, such as kaolinite, since they become mixed with other clay minerals during transport and deposition.

Most of the clay rocks that we find in the stratigraphic column were laid down in the sea, and in many cases the original clay minerals have changed their chemical composition with time as a result of being buried and heated deep in the Earth. The main effect of these changes is to increase the amount of illite at the expense of montmorillonite, and to a lesser extent of kaolinite, so that older clays tend to be richer in illite (Figure 25).

4.2 British clays and bricks

Much of the UK is underlain by pre-Carboniferous rocks, and many of these strata have been strongly folded and metamorphosed. Although many of these rocks were originally deposited as clays, they have been metamorphosed to slates, which contain few unaltered clay minerals, and so are no longer suitable for brick-making. Most of our brick-making rocks are therefore found in the younger geological formations, where clays have been compacted but not recrystallized.

Some of the more important clay rocks used for bricks are shown in Table 11. The names used in the first column of this table are the same as on the *Postcard Geological Map*.

Table 11 Most important clay-bearing strata of Britain

Local name of clay	Geological age	Date of rock/Ma	% of UK clay output	Where formed	Main clay minerals
alluvium, glacial clay	Recent Pleistocene	0.01 2	17	rivers, ice	various
ball clay, London Clay	Tertiary	38 55	4	rivers	kaolinite
Gault Clay, Weald Clay	Cretaceous	135	3	marine and estuaries	illite and montmorillonite
Kimmeridge, Oxford and Lias Clays	Jurassic	180	32	marine and estuaries	
Keuper Marl	Triassic	225	5	desert lakes	illite
Etruria Marl	Permian	280	5	lakes	
Coal Measures	Carboniferous	345	33	swamps, deltas	illite, kaolinite

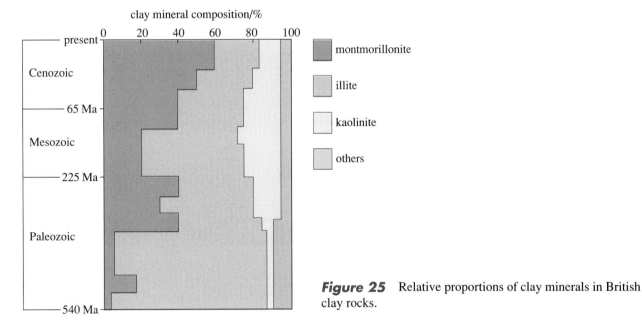

Figure 25 Relative proportions of clay minerals in British clay rocks.

There are three main sources of sedimentary clay used by industry: Carboniferous clays and shales from the Coal Measures, used largely for bricks in all the UK coalfields; the Oxford Clay of Jurassic age, which is traditionally the main brick-making clay of much of southern England; and a variety of smaller superficial deposits of Pleistocene and Recent age, found in other lowland areas of Britain.

Question 14

(a)   Where in the UK is there unlikely to be an abundant supply of brick clay in the solid rocks (see *Postcard Geological Map*)?

(b)   Why might superficial clays formed during the last glacial period be less satisfactory than Carboniferous clays as the basis for a *large-scale* brick-making industry?

4.2.1 Brick-making

Bricks were introduced to this country by the Romans, and during the Middle Ages they began to be used in churches and large important buildings. After the great fire of London (1666), when so much of the timber-built city was destroyed, bricks became the favoured material for rebuilding instead of wood. With the great increase in building accompanying the Industrial Revolution, bricks became the dominant material in our cities. In the last 50 years, concrete and other cement-based materials have displaced bricks in many places such as factories, bridges, and also houses. It seems likely that the overall share of the building market occupied by bricks will continue to decline.

Most clays will make reasonable bricks, but if they are to be used on the outside of buildings, it is important that they are not too porous (so as to minimize frost damage), and are of uniform and attractive appearance. Clay is dug from the quarry, ground and mixed with just enough water to allow it to be extruded or pressed to form the so-called 'green' bricks. These are slowly dried, releasing most of the water, and then they are fired in a kiln to a temperature of 1 000–1 200 °C.

At such temperatures the clay undergoes a type of metamorphism: all the water in the clay minerals is driven off, the structure of the clay minerals breaks down, and new **anhydrous minerals** (literally minerals 'without water'), stable at high temperatures, are formed. For example, kaolinite breaks down to form aluminosilicates such as the mineral **mullite** (Figure 22b), and quartz, by a **dehydration** reaction (a reaction in which water is expelled from the structure of the mineral):

$$3Al_2Si_2O_5(OH)_4 = Al_6Si_2O_{13} + 4SiO_2 + 6H_2O \qquad (4.3)$$

$$\text{kaolinite} \qquad \text{mullite} \quad \text{quartz} \quad \text{water}$$

After firing, the brick contains an interlocking network of long, thin mullite crystals, quartz and some supercooled liquid (glass), which make the brick hard and strong.

Have you ever thought why dark grey or muddy brown wet clay gives bright 'brick red' bricks, tiles or clay pipes after firing? The reason is that virtually all natural clays contain iron as oxides and hydroxides, and iron can exist in two different states. In the iron(II) state (the reduced or ferrous state) it forms a series of dark grey oxides and hydroxides, which give the dark colours to many sediments. After firing in air the iron in the clay oxidizes to the iron(III) state (the oxidized or ferric state), forming the red–brown iron oxide, hematite. (Hematite is also responsible for the red colour of the sand-stone sample in the Rock Kit, though there it was formed by oxidation of iron-bearing minerals in a hot desert environment.) Some-times you can break a bright red brick to find a dark grey centre inside; this is because during firing the outside of the brick recrystallized and sealed out the oxy-gen before all the iron in the centre had been oxidized.

There are many other minor metal constituents in naturally occurring clay, such as Ca^{2+}, Na^+, K^+, and these tend to act as 'fluxes' during firing; that is, they cause melting by forming silicate liquids, which greatly speed up the alteration of the clay minerals of the green brick, and help to bind the new high-temperature minerals together. On cooling, this silicate liquid forms a glassy coat to the particles, which helps to form a hard brick. The amount of liquid has to be kept very small during firing, so that the bricks do not 'sag', and come out of the kiln in irregular shapes, or — in the extreme case — fuse together. You may have seen dark grey–blue bricks used in places like railway bridges, where high strength is required. These so-called 'engin-eering' bricks have a smooth glassy appearance, and are produced by firing to a higher temperature where considerable melting of the clay under reduc-ing conditions occurs (hence the colour). This produces a much stronger brick for severe load-bearing structures. As these bricks have had all their pores sealed by the glass, and are quite impermeable, they were sometimes used for the 'damp-proof' course in nineteenth-century houses. Old bricks fired at low temperatures may remain porous and permeable, which can allow damp to penetrate through walls. If a brick is permeable, a drop of water put onto its surface will disappear into the brick; with impermeable engineering bricks, water will always stay on the surface.

There are also non-metallic elements present in most natural clays, such as sulphur (S), chlorine (Cl) and fluorine (F). During firing, these elements may be driven off as volatile compounds, together with the water. Often the effects of these emissions can be seen near kilns where clay is fired — for example, the etching of glass windows by fluorine compounds. There has been much concern that some of the emissions from brickworks have been responsible for fluorine-related diseases in cattle in surrounding areas.

4.2.2 Brick production and uses of bricks

The output of bricks in the UK changed dramatically during the period 1948–97; its relationship to housebuilding is shown in Figure 26.

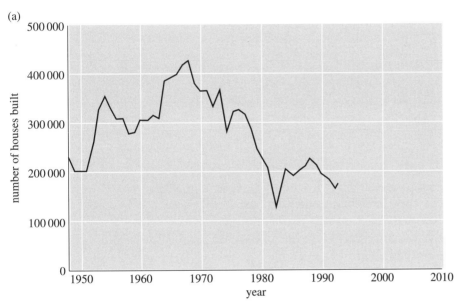

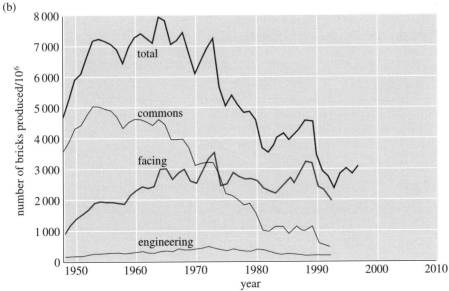

Figure 26 Bricks for the building industry: (a) houses built in the UK 1948–93; (b) brick production in the UK 1948–97 (facing bricks are for the outside of buildings; commons are lower-quality bricks used internally).

○ How does the total output of bricks in 1990 compare with that in the 1960s?

○ Total output in 1990 was about 4 *billion* (4×10^9), much less than the average of 7 billion for the 1960s, with a peak output of almost 8 billion in 1965.

○ What is the main use for bricks today, and what is the main influence on brick production?

○ The main use is housebuilding, and so, of course, the demand is extremely dependent on the number of houses being built, which has diminished greatly since the 1960s. This is an excellent example of the variability of demand for building materials.

Question 15

(a) If all the bricks produced in 1965 were made into a 'single skin', 1.6 m-high, garden wall (1 brick thick and 20 bricks high), how many kilometres long would it be? (Assume a brick is 240 mm long in the wall, including the mortar.)

(b) If all the clay for the bricks produced in 1990 came from a single pit, working a bed of clay 20 m thick, what is the area of clay pit that would have to be dug each year? (Assume that the density of the clay in the ground is the same as the finished brick, that there is no waste, and that the dimensions of a brick are 220 mm × 100 mm × 75 mm.)

It is clear from Figure 26 that there is close correlation between house-building and overall brick production. In the short term, with the downturn in the housebuilding market, bricks in the early 1990s were in decline; but there has also been a long-term drop in production due to a falling demand for commons, the cheaper bricks used for internal walls covered by a decorative finish. These have been in steady decline from a peak in the mid-1950s, and were almost unaffected by the late-1980s building boom. Engineering bricks form only a very small part of the market, and are used for situations where structural strength or water-resistance is required.

○ What might be the explanation for the changes in production of the different types of brick shown in Figure 26b?

○ The most likely reason is that there has been substitution of common bricks by cheaper cement-based blocks, a good example of economic substitution.

Also, because higher standards of thermal insulation are now specified in building regulations, lightweight blocks made from a variety of other materials are used today for the inner 'skin' of house walls. These blocks can be less than half the density of bricks, because they have a high porosity, and it is these air spaces, which give better thermal insulation properties. Many of these materials can be made into blocks that are about six times the volume of a brick; a wall made of these blocks is therefore much quicker and cheaper to build than one made of bricks.

From the data in Figure 26 alone, an alternative explanation could be that there is a shortage of brick-making clays, due to exhaustion of supply. For the answer to this let us look at what used to be the most concentrated area of brick-making in the UK, which is based on a layer of rock which runs though the heart of Milton Keynes; it is the geological formation on which the Open University campus is built.

4.2.3 Making bricks from Oxford Clay

The Oxford Clay is of Jurassic age, just less than 180 Ma old, and forms the south-eastern (upper) part of the pale blue band on the *Postcard Geological Map*, which runs in a south-west to north-east band from Dorset to Yorkshire. It is at its thickest between Peterborough and Milton Keynes (Figure 27).

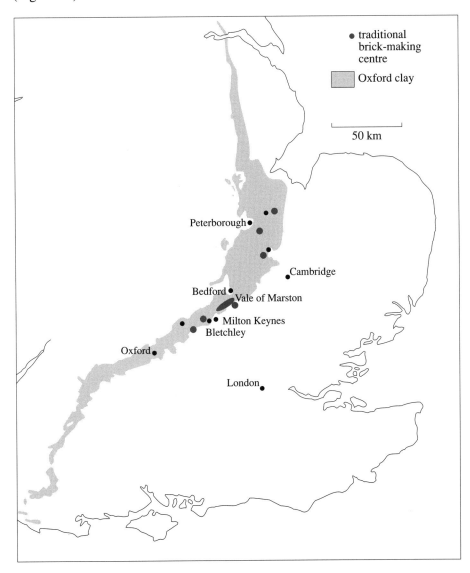

Figure 27 The outcrop of the Oxford Clay, showing the traditional centres of brick-making.

The Oxford Clay is particularly suitable for making bricks for several reasons. It is a fairly thick bed (about 20 m) of uniform quality, it has a very long outcrop, and it is easily accessible beneath a thin soil. The clay itself is easily excavated and crushed, and it needs only a little more water to be added to the 20% it contains naturally to make it workable for extrusion as 'green' bricks. However, its main attraction is that it contains considerable quantities of finely dispersed petroleum hydrocarbons, which provide a kind of 'built in' fuel for the firing. (In Block 4 *Energy 1* you will see that this is similar to rocks that have acted as source rocks for North Sea oil.)

One of the major costs of brick-making is the fuel needed for drying and firing, and whereas normal clays need about 250–300 kg of coal per thousand bricks, Oxford Clay needs only about 70 kg of coal. After initial firing to raise the temperature of the kiln, the hydrocarbons begin to burn, and thereafter the bricks are virtually self-firing. Huge factories were established along the outcrop of the Oxford Clay, with cheaply run coal-fired kilns (chambers filled with bricks, which are sealed and then fired) for supplying bricks to the expanding urban areas, especially greater London. One problem with old-fashioned coal-firing is that the temperature and atmosphere in the kiln are variable, making it very difficult to put all the bricks through exactly the same firing conditions, and so the bricks can be of variable appearance. This was not a problem for commons, but is vital for facings.

In recent years the bricks produced from the Oxford Clay have become less popular, because many architects now specify higher-quality facing bricks, which are more easily produced in continuous gas-fired tunnel kilns than by the batch process. In gas-fired kilns the bricks pass slowly through on a trolley and the temperature can be more easily controlled to give all the bricks a more uniform appearance. So the changing needs of the building industry, a fall in demand for cheap bricks, and higher thermal insulation standards, have all been important in the relative decline of brick-making from the Oxford Clay, and the subsequent closure of many brickworks (such as the one shown in Plate 21b).

4.3 Past and future use of bricks; reserves of brick clays

Apart from bricks used for housing, the Victorians used huge quantities of bricks, many of them engineering bricks, for other major constructional work such as warehouses, factories (Plate 20), mill chimneys, embankment walls and, especially, railway viaducts (Figure 28). Many of these bricks were made from Carboniferous clays and shales, which were abundant around all the industrial centres in the British coalfields (Table 11).

Another major factor in the decline of the brick industry has been the substitution of other materials for bricks in large structures. Before the 1950s most housing and commercial buildings still used brick for structural (load-bearing) walls. But modern high-rise flats and offices now use a steel or concrete

Figure 28 Stockport viaduct (550 m long, 32 m high, 27 arches) — one of the largest brick structures in the world. It was first built in 21 months in 1839–40, using 11 million bricks and nearly a third of a million tonnes of sandstone slabs, and carried the Manchester to Crewe railway line over the Mersey gap. The whole structure was doubled in size in 1887–9 by building an identical structure alongside, to widen the line to four tracks.

frame to carry the structural load, and often have walls of glass, concrete, or some other non-load-bearing material. When bricks are used in such buildings, they often form only a thin decorative 'skin', one brick thick. Motorways, today's equivalents of the Victorian railways, use very few bricks. Bridges, retaining walls, and often the motorway itself, are made largely of concrete, and airport runways also require huge quantities of concrete (Table 6).

Substitution has taken place with the use of brick-making clays for another important product: roof tiles. We saw in Section 2.8 that with the coming of the railways in the 1830s, slate from North Wales, Cornwall and the Lake District became the normal roofing material for houses all over the country; similarly, tiles based on brick clays were also widely distributed. But today few houses are roofed with natural slates or clay tiles. They have both been replaced by cheaper cement-based tiles; old-fashioned slates and clay tiles are now expensive and quite hard to obtain. Some recent buildings have even abandoned (sensible) sloping roofs almost entirely in favour of flat concrete roofs, waterproofed with bitumen.

A similar contraction in the demand for brick-making clays has occurred below ground. Victorian sewers were invariably brick lined, and smaller underground water and drainage pipes often used earthenware pipes made from brick clay. Today, large-diameter waste and water pipes to be laid underground are usually either made of concrete or cast iron, whereas smaller-diameter pipes are often made of plastic. This leaves the housing market as the largest user of bricks, but even here, not only are many inner walls no longer made of bricks, but modern houses are built on concrete rather than brick foundations.

Finally, to return to the question of reserves: is there still plenty of clay for bricks in the ground, in spite of settlements like Milton Keynes having been built on the Oxford Clay, so sterilizing some of the reserves?

○ Look again at Figure 27. How many square kilometres are covered by the outcrop of the Oxford Clay between, say, Milton Keynes and the Wash?

○ The outcrop is about 100 km long, and on average about 25 km wide, so occupies about 2 500 km².

Question 16

Assume that the Oxford Clay can be worked to a depth of 20 m, and that about 30% of the land could be made available for clay extraction.

(a) How many cubic metres of Oxford Clay could be produced for brick-making?

(b) If the proportion of UK bricks made from the Oxford Clay stays at about 30% (Table 11), how long will supplies last at the 1990 rate of production? (Assume that 1 m³ of clay in the ground can produce about 400 bricks.)

So even if many of the assumptions made above are on the optimistic side, shortage of supply of brick clay is not likely here in the foreseeable future. Elsewhere there are also vast reserves in the shales and mudstones of Carboniferous rocks, and many of these are readily available near the surface. In fact they are often exposed when coal is extracted by opencast methods.

4.4 Landfilling

Waste has been discarded in a relatively uncontrolled manner since the earliest times. Prehistoric middens, with their discarded food and domestic utensils, are of interest to archaeologists, since they provide valuable information on diet and living conditions. During Victorian times, before the development of modern mains sewerage systems, simple 'earth closets' were common (the water closet was invented by Thomas Crapper, and not widely available until the end of the nineteenth century). The contents of earth closets were removed during the hours of darkness (hence the name 'night soil'), and this material from the growing conurbations of Victorian Britain was disposed of locally. On Tyneside, for instance, it was deposited in steep-sided valleys draining to the Tyne in such large amounts that the valleys were filled in. Subsequently, when this ground was developed, the night soil was found — as might be expected — to be a poor foundation for buildings, which consequently suffered subsidence.

Today, this would not qualify as landfill, although in many parts of the world similar conditions still exist. **Landfilling** is now defined as 'the controlled deposit of waste on land, in a manner such that pollution or harm is negligible'. Since the 1970s, efforts have been made in the UK to ensure that the deposit of waste to land has a minimal effect on the environment, and legislation has increasingly been used to back this up.

Traditionally, domestic wastes were disposed of locally, often into small quarries from which stone had been taken to build the nearby towns. However, many of these small quarries have now been filled, especially ones near to the large centres of population, so that other solutions to waste disposal have to be sought. In some places, domestic wastes are incinerated, but landfill is still the most popular method, and, after separation of appropriate matter for recycling, many millions of cubic metres of waste are deposited in landfill sites annually.

Landfilling presents a number of potential environmental challenges, notably litter production, odour and traffic movements. Of longer-term significance, however, are the problems associated with **leachate** and landfill gas. Leachate is the liquid that seeps through a landfill, mainly from rainwater falling on the site, but also including moisture from the waste itself, and potential seepages from any groundwater that comes into contact with waste. Leachate can extract undesirable substances from the waste, and is a potential threat to water supplies (Figure 12).

Domestic and industrial waste production in the UK

It has been estimated that an average family generates each year about 1 tonne of solid domestic waste, including: five trees as paper, 175 food cans, 225 drinks cans, 112 kg of plastic and 267 glass bottles or jars. (Because much of it is of very low density, it has been estimated that this waste from an average family would occupy about six small 'garden sheds'.) In total, waste from domestic dustbins amounts to about 20 million tonnes a year, and industrial and commercial waste total about 80 million tonnes a year (not counting quarrying and mining).

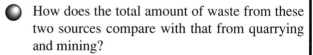 How does the total amount of waste from these two sources compare with that from quarrying and mining?

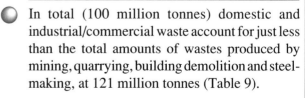 In total (100 million tonnes) domestic and industrial/commercial waste account for just less than the total amounts of wastes produced by mining, quarrying, building demolition and steel-making, at 121 million tonnes (Table 9).

Most domestic waste (85%) and much commercial and industrial waste is buried in landfill sites (Block 1, Section 4).

Landfill gas is a by-product of the bacterial degradation of putrescible matter in landfills. It mainly consists of methane and carbon dioxide, plus traces of other (mainly organic) vapours and gases.

Only completely inert waste will not give rise to leachate and landfill gas, but very few wastes are genuinely inert. Construction and demolition wastes were thought to be inert, but, because of timber, paper, plastics and other degradable materials that are inevitably found in these wastes, even these give off both leachate and landfill gas, although much less than household waste with its higher organic content.

In the past, little regard was paid to leachate or gas control when waste was deposited on land. Leachate was generally assumed to percolate down to the water table; in doing so, it becomes *attenuated*, a term that includes dilution and the complex natural physical, chemical and microbiological processes that act on leachate to reduce its noxious qualities. This approach is known as *dilute and disperse* and, in the UK until the mid-1980s, considerable reliance was placed on this method of dealing with leachate. However, there are uncertainties about the rate of attenuation, depending on the waste and the properties of the rock strata, and the prevailing hydrogeological conditions around the site.

Further, with the 'dilute and disperse' approach, landfill gases (potentially both explosive and asphyxiating) may migrate off-site through porous strata or other pathways such as underground service pipes, and a number of incidents involving migration of gas from landfill sites occurred in the 1980s.

'Dilute and disperse' has now been superseded by a *containment* principle for all wastes apart from those considered to be inert. Containment involves restricting the movement of leachate and landfill gas to the site itself by means of a specially formed impermeable lining system to provide a basal

Landfill containment liners

There is general recognition by the regulatory body responsible for protecting underground and surface water quality — the Environment Agency — that landfill sites that accept non-inert waste must be constructed with impermeable liners designed to:

> prevent the escape of leachate to underground or surface waters;

> prevent underground water percolating into the waste to produce more leachate;

> control the migration of landfill gas.

Two types of lining materials are used to seal sites before filling begins:

(a) Plastic sheeting, usually high-density poly-ethylene (HDPE), 2 mm or more in thickness, called a **geomembrane**. The HDPE arrives at the site in rolls about 7 m wide and up to 100 m long; the sheet material has to be joined by special heat welding techniques on-site by skilled technicians (Plate 21a).

(b) Clay, 1 m thick, and carefully compacted by special machinery until it is effectively impermeable. This type of liner is called a **mineral liner**, and is the same basic technique used 200 years ago to make canals watertight with a 'puddled' layer of clay.

Since landfill sites are sizeable operations, substantial quantities of materials are required. Typically, a new landfill site might occupy some 10 hectares. This requires $100\,000\,m^2$ of HDPE (at, say, £5 per m^2) or $100\,000\,m^3$ of clay (the cost of which depends on whether suitable clay is present at the site or has to be brought in).

These two types of liner may behave differently under a pile of waste many metres in thickness and many tonnes in weight. A split geomembrane or a dried-out clay mineral liner could allow leakage of leachate. Thus, it is now usual to attempt to get the 'best of both worlds' by specifying a composite liner, consisting of a mineral liner overlain by an HDPE geomembrane, but this extra security against leakage of leachate and migration of landfill gas comes at a price. In these modern engineered landfill sites, the cost of waste disposal has risen substantially.

layer on which the waste is placed. By making the base of the site truly impermeable, all leachate can be collected on-site and treated before disposal. The liner will also ensure that no gas can escape; it is either vented to the atmosphere via pipes built into the waste or, if sufficient volumes are produced, collected for use as a fuel (see box on landfill liners).

Brickpits in the vale of Marston, east of Milton Keynes

Clay is always an impermeable material, and so low-lying brickpits will tend to flood (Plate 21b). Some Oxford Clay pits are now used for watersports, or wet wildlife sites, rather like old gravel pits. But old brickpits in the Oxford Clay are now becoming important sites for the disposal of domestic wastes.

● What characteristics of the brickpits in the Oxford Clay do you think would make them suitable for waste disposal?

___

● Some of them must be large, having produced the clay for many tens of millions of bricks (Table 11, Figure 26). Also, clay is readily available to make a mineral liner to contain leachate, and apart from the liner, the clay itself is naturally impermeable.

In the early 1990s in the Vale of Marston (Figure 27) there was a total of about $84 \times 10^6 \, \text{m}^3$ of available space (void) in the ground licensed for landfill, with a possibility of a further $161 \times 10^6 \, \text{m}^3$.

Several of these old brickpits are receiving 5.5 million tonnes of waste per year, including domestic wastes from as far away as London (80 km), and Bristol (150 km). Each day a 'round robin' train arrives from three locations in the Bristol–Bath area, bringing 560 t of domestic waste.

The wastes are compacted, covered with a layer of impermeable clay (Plate 21b) to form a rainproof capping, and then as the rubbish slowly decomposes, the gas given off is collected for use as fuel. Landfill gas is about 60% methane, and so has a high calorific value; in this way, each tonne of waste produces more energy than if it were burned.

The vale of Marston box demonstrates that a large hole in the ground, can itself be a very valuable physical resource, sometimes *more* valuable than the material that was extracted. In many cases, extraction of low-cost building materials today is combined with controlled landfill, so that the visual impact of the quarrying is minimized, and the land restored as extraction takes place.

4.5 Clays and subsidence

There is another important environmental aspect of clays and building: shrinkage of clays causes building subsidence. This was especially noticeable in the series of hot dry summers in the late 1970s and 1980s in areas of southern England where houses have been built on solid clay (see box opposite).

Question 17 _____

(a) Why are you not likely to suffer from subsidence if your house is built on a sandy soil?

(b) Which clays in the stratigraphic column would you expect to be most susceptible to this shrinkage and why (Figure 25 and Table 11)?

(c) Use the *Postcard Geological Map* to decide which clay is especially likely to cause subsidence problems because of its *geographical* position?

One response to this problem is to dig deeper foundations for houses in areas where the underlying clay could shrink. If a house sits on concrete foundations that penetrate deeper into the soil than the zone that may dry out, there should be no subsidence, even in the hottest weather.

House subsidence on major clay formations

Most clay rocks contain a high proportion of natural water (up to 40%), filling all the minute pore spaces between the mineral grains, but because these spaces are so small, water cannot pass through the rock; it is impermeable. Clay topsoils may dry out in a long hot summer, shrinking as they lose water (a process similar to water loss by compaction shown in Figure 6e), and develop cracks in the surface layer.

However, if the ground is also being dried out at depth by tree roots — that is, the underlying clay is being dewatered — the clay can lose enough water in a long, hot summer for it to shrink enough to cause part of the building to settle or **subside**, especially if the house foundations are shallow (Figure 29). Cracks may then develop in the building, requiring expensive remedial work to underpin the foundations. In some cases it is possible to stop the damage by cutting down the tree, and so allow the clay below the house to rehydrate. However, if the tree has been there a long time, rehydration of the clay as it reabsorbs water and swells up can itself cause further ground movements and damage to the house, a process known as **heave**.

If you have trees in the garden, particularly the ubiquitous *Cyprus leylandii*, you will know that the ground around the base of the tree is often much drier than the rest of the garden, since it transpires (loses water vapour via its leaves) all year round. The worst trees for causing subsidence are ones that transpire large quantities of water, such as willows or poplars. The moral of this story is: don't plant large, thirsty trees near your house, or anyone else's.

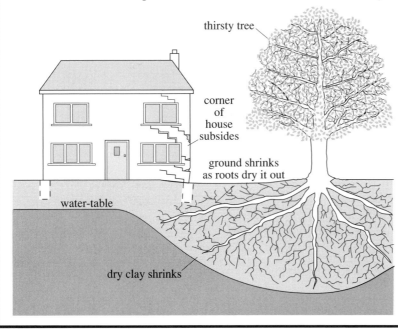

thirsty tree

corner
of
house
subsides

ground shrinks
as roots dry it out

water-table

dry clay shrinks

Figure 29 Subsidence due to clay shrinkage caused by a nearby tree. Usually one corner of the house sinks, causing structural damage.

4.6 Clays for specialist uses

So far, we have considered only clays that can be dug out of the ground and used in bulk for making bricks. However, the whole of the pottery industry is based on clay, from the most delicate china, through sanitary ware (basins, sinks, etc.) to large-diameter earthenware drainage pipes. Many different clays are used for these purposes. For example, the pottery industry of the Stoke-on-Trent area was originally established using Carboniferous clays and shales. Iron-free clays that have had their iron washed out by natural processes have always been in great demand because when they are fired they do not turn dark shades of red and brown. Some of the clays that occur just below coal seams are almost iron-free; they are called 'seatearths' or 'fireclays'. They are in fact 'fossil soils', from which all the iron was leached out when they were exposed to tropical weathering at the Earth's surface in Carboniferous times. Some of these clays have been widely used for earthenware (mugs, plates) and sanitary ware, but they contain other impurities, which make them unsuitable for the finest china and porcelain.

Other clays have also been important resources in the UK in the past. For example, in the Midland Valley of Scotland, Carboniferous clay rocks known as oil shales were quarried and heated to collect petroleum. There are still huge resources of these rocks in the ground, but they are of no economic interest today, as petroleum can be obtained more cheaply from other sources.

4.6.1 Montmorillonite clays

Clays formed largely of montmorillonite are too plastic to make good brick clays, but they have the property of being able to absorb large amounts of water (Figure 24), which makes them valuable materials for many other purposes.

Montmorillonite clays rich in calcium can absorb oil and grease, and were traditionally used for cleaning ('fulling') wool, which gave them their common name 'fuller's earth'. Places such as Bletchley and Bletchingly are called after such 'bleaching earths', where they have been worked since Roman times. More recently, another application of these adsorbent clays is in materials like cat litter. Britain is still a major producer of fuller's earth, with an annual output of a quarter of a million tonnes.

The clay mineral montmorillonite comes in another form: sodium montmorillonite, called **bentonite**, which has a truly remarkable property: it is able to absorb up to *15 times its own volume of water* (calcium montmorillonite can expand by only about 30% in water). Bentonite acts in water like this: the clay disperses to form a suspension of small plates, which carry positive charges on their edges, and negative charges on their surfaces, where the surface charges are partly balanced by the sodium ions present. When the suspension is allowed to stand undisturbed, edges of plates become attracted to faces to form a more electrically balanced open structure, within which large volumes of water are 'trapped' (Figure 30). This forms a jelly-like mass (a gel), which can soon be transformed to a liquid by shaking or stirring, but it will 'gel' again when it is left to stand. Such gel-to-liquid materials are said to be **thixotropic**, and are widely used in industry. Non-drip paint is probably the most familiar product using bentonite, but it is also used as 'finings' to clear beer of sediment.

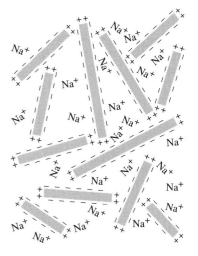

Figure 30 Bentonite crystals in water: plates of charged clay particles have formed an open structure held together by opposing charges, trapping water in this thixotropic 'gel'.

4.6.2 China clay from Devon and Cornwall

Although not really a building material, the **china clay** (kaolin) industry of south-west England exploits one of the most important mineral resources of the UK; after oil, it is the country's most valuable mineral export. In 1990, about 3 million tonnes were produced here, worth over £200m, and more than 2.5 million tonnes of this was exported. The UK is the major European producer, accounting for about 60% of EU output. World production is now about 20 million tonnes, of which nearly half is from the USA. Up to the Second World War, the UK was the world's leading producer of kaolin at 700 000 tonnes a year, and about half of this was exported to the USA. At that time it cost almost exactly half as much to send Cornish kaolin across the Atlantic by ship to north-eastern USA (£0.61 per tonne) as it did to rail freight American kaolin there north from Georgia. After the Second World War, the USA soon became a net exporter of kaolin, and now exports 2 million tonnes a year, nearly as much as the UK.

China clay (rock) is made of the mineral kaolinite, named after the Chinese mountain Kaoling, where a pure white clay was first worked to make high-quality porcelain about 500AD. In 1746, deposits of kaolin were discovered by a Plymouth chemist, William Cookworthy, and soon afterwards the famous potters Wedgwood, Spode and Minton took leases in Cornwall to secure supplies for their newly developed English porcelain and fine china works. It was taken from Cornwall in ships, and then by barge and canal to Staffordshire; the vessels returned to Cornwall with a cargo of coal. This new source of employment in china clay pits was most welcome in the late nineteenth century because large numbers of miners were out of work following the closure of the Cornish tin-mining enterprises. The china clay industry is still one of the south-west's major employers.

The china clay occurs only on some of the granite outcrops in Cornwall and Devon (Figure 31). The china clay deposits formed where acid water penetrated the granite along cracks, altering potassium feldspar to kaolinite. (The reaction is shown as Equation 4.2 in Section 4.1.) There is evidence that at least some of this chemical alteration of the feldspar began in late Carboniferous times (300 Ma) by hot waters associated with the cooling of the granite. The final formation of the kaolinite took place much later during weathering of the granite under sub-tropical conditions, deep below the surface, in early Tertiary times (about 50 million years ago), probably under conditions similar to those that formed Carboniferous 'fossil soils', the seatearth clays used for making cheaper crockery and sanitary ware.

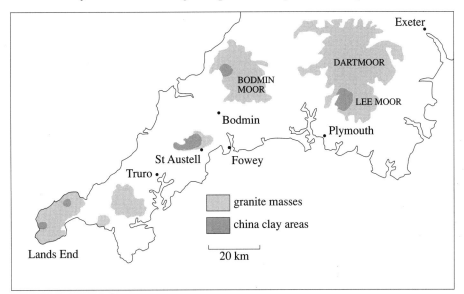

Figure 31 China clay deposits in Cornwall and Devon.

The formation of kaolinite has been compared to the preparation of filter coffee, where the percolating acid water is the boiling water, the partially decomposed granite is the analogue of the fresh coffee grounds, and the kaolinite represents the depleted coffee grounds after percolation. The coffee we drink, is, of course, the analogue of the potassium and dissolved silica removed by the streams draining the area, and ending up in the sea (Equation 4.2).

The china clay occurs in pockets in the top of the granite, the best material occurring where the original granite had a low iron content. This kaolinite is a residual clay mineral deposit, still remaining in its place of formation.

⬤   Would you expect this kaolinite to be pure?

⬤   No. As it came from decomposition of the feldspar in the granite, other minerals that were present in the original rock, and not subject to decomposition by weathering, will still be present. These are chiefly quartz and mica.

China clay is extracted in large open pits by high-pressure water hoses, which wash away the rotted granite; where the feldspar has been decomposed, the granite crumbles easily. This slurry is channelled out of the pit, and the clay is separated from the other minerals of the granite by being passed through a series of settling tanks, where quartz and mica drop out. Finally, the clay is washed, filtered and dried, to give a brilliant white, very fine-grained powder.

The chief use of china clay today is as a filler and surface coating in the production of high-grade paper (paper can be almost 30% by weight kaolinite), which accounts for about 50% of worldwide output. Being a very fine-grained white inert powder, it is also used as a filler and bulking agent in a wide variety of modern materials: plastics, paints, pharmaceuticals, fertilizers, etc. A relatively small amount is still used to make the highest-quality china and porcelain.

4.7 Recycled wastes as building materials: two examples

Wastes from china clay production

China clay is an unusual clay deposit because the kaolinite itself only forms about 12% of the material extracted, the rest being chiefly quartz (50%), mica (12.5%), decomposed granite fragments (12.5%) and overburden (13%); all of these have to be disposed of. The tradition has been to tip this waste, forming huge white hills, known locally as the 'Cornish Alps' (Figure 32). Today, opinions differ about these hills: some argue that they are a sign of mining devastation, which spoils the environment, and so should be put back into old workings; others say that they are a local feature, which adds character and interest to the area, and hence should be preserved, and planted to make them a permanent landscape feature. Many of the present-day workings return the waste materials to the quarries, so that these waste heaps are the legacy of earlier exploitation. In earlier times the local rivers 'ran white' due to clay escaping from the clay separation processes.

○ How much waste from the UK china clay industry is produced each year, and why can it not all be used?

○ About 25 million tonnes (3 million tonnes of china clay represent only 12% of the material extracted). This represents about 25% of the total output of the country's sand and gravel pits, but is remote from centres of population.

These wastes have been used locally to make cement blocks for housebuilding for many years, but local demand for blocks is limited. Transport costs have so far proved to be too high to supply markets further than about 60 km away, and so consumption of these wastes is only running at about 5% of their production (Table 9).

Figure 32 Waste hills from the china clay works in Cornwall: the 'Cornish Alps.' A flooded china clay pit can be seen to the upper left of the photograph.

Possible recycling of industrial wastes: burgy and PFA

Another example of a waste that may have potential for reclamation and recycling — burgy — also illustrates the changing approach to industrial waste. Recycling and reclamation are often used as though they have the same meaning. However, *reclamation* is best used simply to describe the collection of materials separated from waste, whereas *recycling* involves rather more, namely the collection and separation of materials from waste to produce a marketable product.

Burgy (sometimes spelt burghy, bergy or burgee) is the waste generated by the grinding and polishing of plate-glass, using sand from the Mersey Estuary as an abrasive to grind glass with rotating cast-iron plates. It is likely, incidentally, that the origin of the word burgy is derived from 'burgoo', which is nautical slang (from the Turkish 'bulgar', meaning crushed grain for a soupy meal or porridge), alluding to the liquid from which burgy is deposited. Burgy consists of grains of quartz (0.002–0.060 mm), plus small amounts of feldspar and iron oxides; the quartz and feldspar are from the Mersey sand, and the iron oxides from oxidized cast-iron from the grinding wheels.

The grinding process took place at the glass manufacturing works at St Helens on Merseyside until the 1960s, when the grinding of plate-glass ceased due to the introduction of float-glass technology. However, wired-glass still requires grinding and polishing, and this process continues at Doncaster using Mersey sand. Over 100 years, extensive 'burgy banks' close to both glass works have accumulated. The Doncaster ones, occupying some 25 hectares and rising some 15 m, form a significant landscape feature.

Burgy arrives from the glass works as a suspension, and, as the water drains away, burgy sediment accumulates on the floor of the lagoon at a rate of 1 000 tonnes a week.

It would clearly be worth while if a use could be found for this waste. The most promising to date involves the use of burgy as a filling material to stabilize old mineworkings, such as those occurring under Bath (Section 2.9). One way of treating these voids in order to provide support for the ground surface, is to fill them with *grout* by pressure injection from the surface. Grout is essentially a mixture of a fine-grained inert material, a filler, bound together by cement. A ratio of 1 part of cement to 9 parts of filler is usually employed; this provides the required strength with the minimum amount of expensive cement. Currently, pulverized fuel ash (PFA, a by-product from coal-fired power stations) is widely used as a filler, but burgy could well be used, either as a partial or a complete substitute for PFA.

Before using burgy for grouting, its basic physical and chemical properties need to be assessed. Chemically, burgy is an inert material, largely quartz, and so it is unlikely to be dissolved by groundwater. Its density is about 1.7 t m^{-3}.

Burgy is likely to behave in the same way as PFA. However, whether or not it becomes a major replacement for PFA in grout will depend on economic and other considerations. Burgy is only available at these two sites, whereas PFA can be obtained nationwide from power stations. Even so, much PFA still finds no market and is tipped (Table 9).

Localized availability is a limitation for all cheap, and therefore very high place value, materials, and even more so for alternative or 'new' materials like burgy, PFA, and china clay wastes. In addition, there is the intangible 'unfamiliarity' or 'resistance to change' factor, which tends to militate against the introduction of all unconventional materials for constructional purposes. To overcome the latter factor, any 'new' material, like burgy, would have to be priced lower than other alternative grouting materials. Furthermore, barriers to change include lack of detailed material specifications, and approved standards and working procedures. This is a major problem when considering the greater use of recycled waste materials in the construction industry.

Note added in 1998 reprinting

The cost of landfill disposal increased in 1996 with the introduction of the landfill tax (Video Band 18). It seems likely that further moves to tax dumping of wastes and even extraction of resources may be implemented.

4.8 Summary of Section 4

1 Clay minerals form a series of complex layered aluminosilicates, whose crystal structure may accommodate varying amounts of water. This gives them several unique properties.

2 The main use for British clays is in bricks for the building industry.

3 Substitution of bricks by concrete and other materials has led to a considerable decline in the quantities of bricks produced since the 1960s.

4 Some clays, such as china clays and montmorillonite, are quarried in large quantities for more specialized uses. China clay is an important raw material export from the UK.

5 Old brickpits are becoming valuable as sites for waste disposal, and wastes from the china clay and other industries are potentially re-usable as building materials.

5 LIMESTONES, CEMENT AND CONCRETE

So far in this Block, the building materials discussed have largely been produced as clastic fragments — pebbles of rock, or grains of resistant minerals like quartz — by the physical process of erosion, or as insoluble weathering products like clay minerals. The next two Sections are concerned with the soluble products of the rock cycle, materials that were formed largely by chemical and biological processes.

⬤ What happened to the calcium, sodium and potassium originally present in the feldspars during chemical weathering of granite (Section 4.1, Figure 23)?

⬤ These elements went into *solution* as ions (Ca^{2+}, Na^+, K^+) in the acid water that broke down the feldspar to form clay minerals.

As you learned in Block 1, once these ions are in solution they will be carried through the hydrological cycle to the sea, where they may be precipitated to form the third major group of sediments, chemical sediments, of which limestones (made up chiefly of the mineral calcite, $CaCO_3$) are the most important. The remains of shelly fossils are frequently found in limestones, often as broken fragments. In fact, biological processes play an important part in the formation of most limestones.

Calcium carbonate, dissolved in seawater, is in equilibrium with dissolved carbon dioxide, calcium ions and bicarbonate ions:

$$Ca^{2+} + 2HCO_3^- = CaCO_3 + H_2O + CO_2 \qquad (5.1)$$

In some places in the sea the concentration of dissolved carbon dioxide is so low that calcium carbonate is precipitated without any biological help. There are many examples in the geological record of limestones, like the Bath Stone in the Rock Kit, where spherical ooids look as though they represent this direct precipitation: concentric layers of calcium carbonate built up around particles rolling around on the sea floor. Precipitation is a process that is more important in the formation of evaporites (see Section 6).

Limestones accumulate on the sea floor, and pure limestone can be almost 100% $CaCO_3$, provided no other sediments were being laid down. Sometimes carbonate sediment forms at the same time as clastic material from the land is accumulating; the result is an impure limestone, such as a sandy limestone.

5.1 British limestones

In the UK there are limestones of various ages, and the most important of these are shown on Figure 33. You should be able to identify each of these on the *Postcard Geological Map*.

The three most important limestones exploited as resources are as follows:

1 Carboniferous limestones are usually well-cemented grey rocks, tough and of very low porosity, of which there is a typical example in the Rock Kit. They occur in thick beds, and have prominent regularly spaced vertical fractures called joints, and so are easily split into blocks for building stone. They are responsible for the spectacular scenery of the Peak District, Mendips and the Yorkshire Dales, and contain most of the

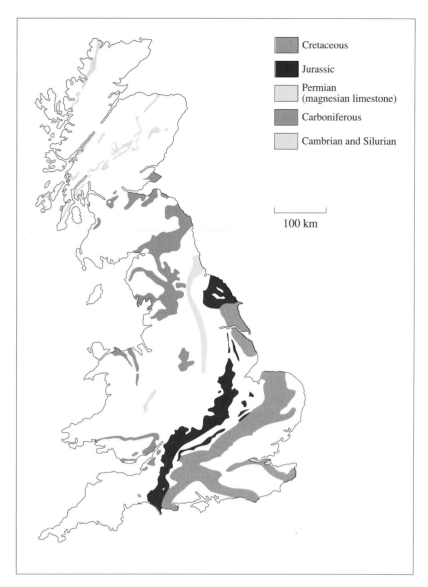

Cretaceous

Jurassic

Permian
(magnesian limestone)

Carboniferous

Cambrian and Silurian

100 km

Figure 33 Geological map of mainland Britain, showing the areas mainly underlain by limestone.

country's 'potholes' and natural cave systems. Most Carboniferous limestone is either fine calcite mud, precipitated from warm shallow seas, or shelly limestone, formed by fragments of animals like shellfish and corals. In places the abundance of fossils suggests that the limestone is the remains of a fossil reef community (Figure 34a). Carboniferous limestone is often very tough, and so is widely used as a roadstone. It is often sufficiently pure calcium carbonate to be used for cement-making (for example, both the limestone quarries in Video Band 5: *Rocks for Roads*). In places it is exceptionally pure and so can be used as a source of calcium carbonate for the chemical industry.

2   Jurassic limestones occur mainly along the length of the Cotswolds; they are generally pale brown, much softer and more porous than Carboniferous limestone. They occur in beds a few metres thick, and are often oolitic, looking rather like fish roe (Figure 34b); the sample in the Rock Kit is typical. They have been widely used for building stones, particularly in the Cotswolds. In some places, such as in Bath and at Portland, they are sufficiently well cemented to be used as good freestones (Video Band 4: *Stones for Building*). They are generally not strong enough and are too porous to make good roadstone. In some places they are used for cement-making.

3   Cretaceous limestones are all varieties of the **Chalk**, which dominates much of the scenery of south-east England, for example the North and

(a)

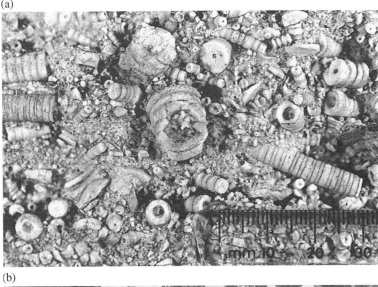

(b)

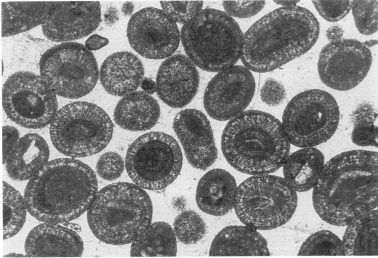

(c)

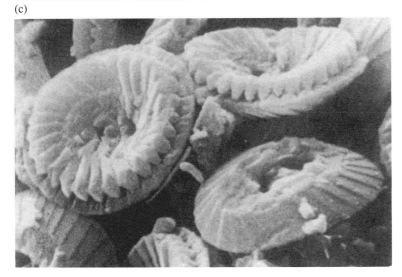

Figure 34 Structure of limestones:
(a) fossiliferous limestone (actual size) of Carboniferous age, Derbyshire; the rock is made up of the broken remains of reef-dwelling animals, crinoids ('sea lilies');
(b) Jurassic oolitic limestone in thin section, magnification × 20 to show concentric layers in ooids;
(c) Cretaceous limestone, Chalk, magnification × 2 000 (electron microscope).

South Downs, white cliffs of Dover, the Needles in the Isle of Wight. In all cases it is very fine-grained, porous, pure white rock, formed from the remains of planktonic organisms, and made up of extremely fine plates of calcite (Figure 34c). Bedding is difficult to see unless there are rows of flint nodules. Chalk itself is usually much too soft to be used as a building stone (except for some well-cemented material called Beer-stone, found in south-west England). It is almost pure calcite, and is widely used in cement-making.

5.2 Cement

5.2.1 Making cement and concrete

The basic feature of cement is that after mixing with water it will eventually set to form a hard rock-like mass, firmly binding together any rock and mineral fragments with which it is mixed. **Mortar**, made from a mixture of cement and sand, bonds the bricks in a wall together, but most cement is mixed with aggregate as well as sand to make concrete, the ubiquitous building material of our age.

After Roman times the secret of cement was lost. It was not until 1756, when John Smeaton built the Eddystone lighthouse (Figure 35) using a mixture of fired ground limestone and clay, which he found would set hard even under water, that cement technology was rediscovered. Cement was patented in 1824 by John Aspdin, who called it Portland cement, because he thought that his cement looked rather like Jurassic limestone from Portland, Dorset, which was then in common use as a building stone. This is the main type of cement used today, and is still called 'OPC' (ordinary Portland cement).

There are three essential ingredients needed to make cement: calcite ($CaCO_3$) from limestone, silica (SiO_2) and alumina (Al_2O_3), as well as a little iron, and all of these can be assembled by mixing limestone and shale. The two rocks are ground together, and then fired in a kiln to a temperature of about 1 400 °C, when first water and then CO_2 are given off, indicating the decomposition of first the shale and then the limestone. The other materials react to produce cement **clinker**. The four most important anhydrous compounds in Portland cement are listed below in decreasing order of abundance. They are represented as mixtures of oxides (you do not need to remember the formulae).

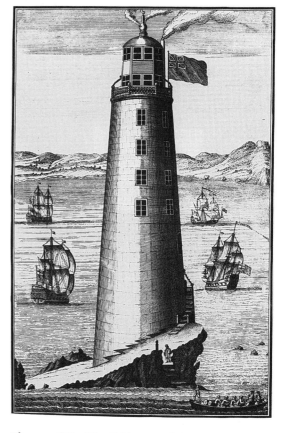

Figure 35 The Eddystone lighthouse built by John Smeaton in 1756.

tricalcium silicate, $3CaO.SiO_2$

dicalcium silicate, $2CaO.SiO_2$

tricalcium aluminate, $3CaO.Al_2O_3$

tetracalcium aluminoferrite, $4CaO.Al_2O_3.Fe_2O_3$

It is clear that the original sedimentary clay minerals (containing water) and calcium carbonate from the limestone have undergone a kind of metamorphism, so that the clinker contains neither water nor carbonates. The cement clinker is then ground to a powder to produce OPC. When cement is mixed with water, new hydrated minerals form, which grow as long crystals, locking the cement and any inert particles present into a hard mass (Figure 36).

It is important to realize that the formation of these new hydrated minerals takes place slowly, and that the cement needs to be kept moist while this is happening. Portland cement begins to harden in a few hours after mixing, largely due to the rapid growth of hydrated tricalcium aluminate (Figure 36a), but the real strength of cement only develops after a few days when the more abundant hydrated tricalcium silicate develops, reaching about 70% of its final strength in a month (Figure 37b). However, cement does not reach its full strength for several years, as the dicalcium silicate hydrates only very

(a) (b) (c)

0.005 mm   0.005 mm   0.005 mm

Figure 36 Growth of cement crystals to make an 'artificial rock': (a) early needles on cement grains; (b) cement grain covered with fibres of gel and two rod-like crystals; (c) final mass of interlocking fibres.

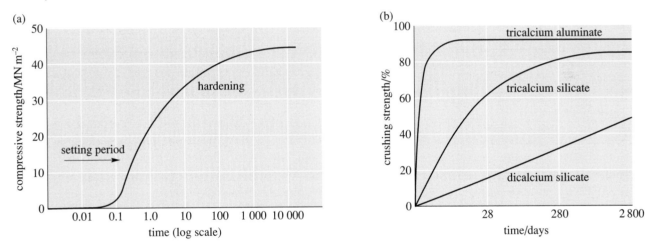

Figure 37 Setting of cement, showing strength increasing with time: (a) gradual build up of crushing strength in cement paste after mixing; time is a log scale, in days, and the vertical linear scale shows strength in compression ($MN\,m^{-2}$; see box overleaf); (b) the crushing strength of the three principal compounds in cement develops at different rates; the strength of each compound is shown as a percentage of its final strength.

slowly (Figure 37b). Just because cement or concrete is 'set', it does not mean you can treat it as fully hardened and ready to be walked or driven over (Figure 37a).

The reactions that occur in the hardening of cement are complex, and *non-reversible*, so that once cement has set, the new hydrated compounds that have formed cannot change back to the anhydrous minerals present in the cement clinker.

A useful analogy for these cement reactions is to think of them as a kind of 'human-driven rock cycle'. To make cement clinker, sedimentary rocks are subjected to conditions equivalent to the metamorphic and igneous part of the rock cycle, and so lose water and CO_2. Adding water to cement powder is comparable to very rapid weathering of igneous rocks: the minerals in the cement become hydrated, in the same way as feldspar does when it weathers to kaolinite. In both cases the high-temperature minerals in igneous rocks or clinker are unstable under the cool wet conditions at the Earth's surface.

Indeed, some of the hydrated minerals formed in set cement are a similar size and shape to clay minerals formed during weathering (cf. Figures 22a and 36).

The compressive strength of building materials

All the building materials described in this Block — stone, brick and concrete — have to support the load of overlying structures: a brick in the bottom of a wall has to carry the weight of the house above it, the foundations of a railway bridge must bear the load of the bridge itself and any trains, and the base of a road must sustain the weight of the rest of the road and the hammering of passing traffic for many years. A vital property of these materials is their ability to resist being crushed — their **crushing** or **compressive strength** — which can be thought of as a pressure, or a *force per unit area*. How is this measured, and what units do we use to compare these different materials?

In Figure 37a the compressive strength of cement was plotted in $MN\,m^{-2}$, millions of newtons per square metre ($10^6\,N\,m^{-2}$). You may see compressive strengths quoted as $N\,mm^{-2}$, which is the same, because there are a million square millimetres in a square metre.

The scientific (SI) unit of force is the **newton (N)**, named after Sir Isaac Newton (and his apple!). It represents the force of gravity acting on the mass of a typical apple, about $0.1\,kg$ ($\frac{1}{4}$ lb). The SI unit of pressure (force per unit area) is the pascal (Pa), the force of a newton acting over a square metre ($1\,Pa \equiv 1\,N\,m^{-2}$). This is much too small a pressure to be useful in testing materials, so compressive or crushing strength is usually measured in units of meganewtons per square metre or newtons per square millimetre.

The crushing strength of rocks varies a great deal, but it is usually high enough not to be a limiting factor for everyday buildings. For example, the crushing strength of a soft limestone or sandstone may be as low as $10–30\,MN\,m^{-2}$, whereas that of a well-cemented sandstone or limestone is typically: $30–50\,MN\,m^{-2}$ (although Carboniferous Limestone may approach $100\,MN\,m^{-2}$), and igneous rocks like fresh granite lie in the range $100–300\,MN\,m^{-2}$.

Crushing strength is most frequently measured on man-made materials such as concrete as a quality control check. At the same time as the concrete is being poured, sample 'cubes' of concrete are cast, allowed to set, and then crushed to destruction in a large press.

⬤ Why is the time after pouring likely to be a very important factor when measuring the crushing strength of concrete test cubes?

⬤ Because the cement continues to gain in strength over many months (Figure 37), so that cubes of the same mix tested at different times after pouring will show a steadily increasing range of values. It is normal to specify a concrete by the strength it has to achieve after 28 days setting, and typical values lie in the range $20–40\,MN\,m^{-2}$. When the test 'cubes' do not come up to strength, concrete used for structural purposes has to be demolished and new material cast.

Large hydraulic presses are used to crush $100\,mm$ cubes of building materials, but it is possible to gain some idea of the strength with which the crystals are held together in a rock or concrete material by applying high pressure to a small area, and seeing if the grains flake off or crush under localized pressure. The point of a hardened steel penknife blade is appropriate to see if a rock or mineral is soft enough to be easily scratched.

⬤ If the area of contact at the point of the blade is $1\,mm^2$, and the applied force is $20\,N$ ($2\,kg$), what pressure will be generated on the rock surface under the blade?

⬤ $20\,N$ ($2\,kg$) applied to $1\,mm^2$ will generate a force of $20\,MN\,m^{-2}$, which is enough to crush a fairly weak sedimentary rock like Chalk.

Rocks that can be easily scratched using light pressure with the point of a penknife will tend to have compressive strengths below about $30\,MN\,m^{-2}$. On the other hand it is difficult to make any impression like this on tough igneous rocks with strengths above $100\,MN\,m^{-2}$.

Have you ever wondered about the crushing strengths of materials used in very tall buildings? You can now apply these techniques to see how the crushing strength of common materials compares with the kinds of pressure likely to be met in buildings.

Question 18

(a)   How many apples (average weight 0.1 kg) would have to be piled up on to a square metre of paving stone to produce a pressure of $1\,MN\,m^{-2}$?

(b)   A stone plinth has a measured crushing strength of $40\,MN\,m^{-2}$, and is to carry a granite column (the density of granite is $2.6\,t\,m^{-3}$). What height of column of $1\,m^2$ cross-section area could be supported on the plinth to just exert a force equivalent to half the crushing strength of the stone? (This would give a safety factor of 100%, since the plinth should be only half way to its point of failure.)

Question 19

(a)   After 3 months, what is the compressive strength of the cement in Figure 37?

(b)   What compound(s) is (are) causing the increase in strength after 1 month?

(c)   How old is the cement before it reaches its full compressive strength, and what is this value?

5.2.2   Geology and raw materials for making cement

In a few places, sediments are found with roughly the correct proportions of minerals present to make these sediments ideal raw materials for making cement.

● What are the elements needed to make the essential compounds in cement clinker?

● From the list of compounds in cement clinker: calcium, silicon, oxygen, aluminium, iron (Section 5.2.1).

Cement stones are impure limestones containing both quartz and clay minerals, and some iron (see Table 12). In practice, there is always some magnesium present, and, of course, water and carbon dioxide too. Sometimes a cement stone consists of thin limestones and shales closely interbedded to give in total the composition needed for cement-making (Figure 52, Block 1). Normally, however, a cement works is built where suitable limestone and clay rock outcrop next to each other. The raw material for the cement kiln is then prepared by mixing the correct proportions of the two rocks together. In the south of England there are many cement works on the edge of the Chalk, where the underlying clay from one end of the quarry is mixed with the Chalk, worked from the other end, to give the raw mix for the cement kiln. The ideal situation occurs where the limestone and shale are of consistent composition, so that preparing a constant chemical mix for the kiln is routine.

Often, the limestone and shale are dug from separate beds in the same quarry, and the composition of one or both is variable; preparing a mix for the kiln is then more difficult. In the limestone quarry shown in Figure 38 at Dunbar, where more than one limestone is worked for cement, wastes are tipped as the working face advances. The land is rapidly restored behind the excavation itself, as part of the quarrying operation, rather like open-cast working of coal.

Table 12   Chemical compositions of rocks used for cement-making (weight per cent)

Rock type	SiO_2	Al_2O_3	Fe_2O_3	CaO	MgO	CO_2	H_2O
cement stone	16.2	4.8	1.6	40.2	2.8	34.2	0.8
limestone	1.2	0.5	0.4	54.0	0.6	43.2	0.7
shale	58.1	22.4	4.0	3.1	2.4	2.6	7.0

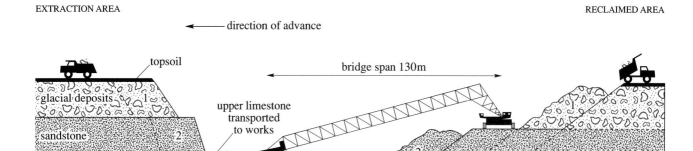

EXTRACTION AREA   RECLAIMED AREA

← direction of advance

Figure 38 Limestones and shales for cement-making: cross-section of a cement quarry near Dunbar, Scotland, where beds of shale and two limestones are worked together (see also Video Band 5). The numbers indicate the blocks of strata before extraction and the corresponding layers of backfill.

Now would be a good time to watch the first two parts of Video Band 5: *Rocks for Roads* (made in 1993), which deals with limestone quarried for cement. The programme was made in 1993.

Video Band 5   Rocks for Roads (First two quarries, Eastgate and Dunbar)

Speakers

Eric Dack	Blue Circle Cement (quarry manager, Eastgate)
Ross Dunn	Blue Circle Cement (general manager, Dunbar)
Alan Ruxton	Blue Circle Cement (quarry manager, Dunbar)

The first two parts of Video Band 5 visit two quarries working Carboniferous Limestone for cement-making. Later the video visits sites where materials are extracted and processed for road-building, and raises more general issues about the resources for road-building in the future. (The programme starts with a few minutes' introduction from all the speakers. We shall come back to that later, in Section 8; for the moment, just watch the first 15 minutes about the two limestone quarries.)

The first quarry is at Eastgate (Plate 22) in Weardale, Durham (just north of the first red blob of igneous rock on the London to Edinburgh route on the *Postcard Geological Map*). The second is at Dunbar,

south-east Scotland (shown on the *Postcard Geological Map* as a speck of Carboniferous, on the North Sea coast due east of Edinburgh).

New terms introduced in this Video Band:

SRC: sulphate-resistant cement, high in iron, used for concrete foundations in areas where the groundwater is acidic, and would be liable to attack ordinary Portland cement (OPC).

'dirty' and 'clean' limestones: ones with, respectively, a lot and a little shaley material (clay minerals) present in addition to calcium carbonate.

bridge conveyor: a large belt conveyor for moving *overburden* (waste above the limestones) and *interburden* (waste shales and sandstones between the limestones) from one side of the quarry to the other (Figure 38).

magnesian limestone: a limestone rich in magnesium carbonate, unsuitable for cement-making.

Several terms are used referring to machinery such as *rope shovel*, etc., which do not concern us.

After viewing the first two parts of Video Band 5, consider the following questions:

○ Would you call the limestone at Eastgate a cement stone, and why is it a difficult rock to use for cement-making?

○ It is almost a cement stone, since only 5% of shale has to be added to it to obtain the required composition for cement-making. The problem is that the rock itself is very variable in chemical composition, so making it difficult to keep a fixed composition for the cement works.

○ Why is the very expensive bridge conveyor justified at Dunbar, and what environmental advantage does it give to the quarry?

○ It is the cheapest way to move large amounts of waste across the quarry (replacing many vehicles) because its high capital cost can be spread over the very long quarry life (50 years). It enables the quarry waste to fill up the old workings continuously, so that there is only a narrow strip of quarry exposed at any one time.

5.2.3 Uses of cement

Mortar for bonding bricks together is prepared by mixing about 1 part by volume of cement powder with 3 to 6 parts of sand, and the minimum amount of water to make the mix workable (often some lime is added for workability). Cement can also be used mixed with sand to produce a thin skin or render, to protect the outside of buildings, particularly ones built with a wooden framework, covered only with galvanized wire mesh. This is a quick if rather fragile technique, used in the USA. But the most important use of cement is for making concrete, where it is used to 'glue' a mixture of sand and rock fragments (aggregate) giving an appearance of artificial sedimentary rock.

5.2.4 Production and consumption of cement

We have already seen that UK brick production has been in decline since the 1960s (Figure 26), and suggested that this was partly because cement-based materials such as cast cement building blocks and concrete were being substituted for brickwork. Figure 39 shows UK cement production; comparison of these two Figures may lend support to this idea.

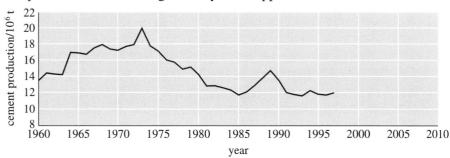

Figure 39 Annual cement production in Britain 1960–97.

Question 20

(a)   Take the values for cement and brick output from Figures 26 and 39 for the start of each decade, and enter them in the first four columns of the two top rows of Table 13.

(b)   How has the ratio of bricks to cement changed with time (bottom row of Table 13), and do these data indicate the replacement (substitution) of bricks by concrete?

(c)   Does the fall in production from 1960 to 1990 (final two columns) agree with your conclusion in part b (take the output in 1960 as 100%)?

Table 13 Brick and cement production 1960–90

	1960	1970	1980	1990	Fall in production 1960–90	% fall in production 1960–90
no. of bricks/10^9						
wt of cement/10^6 tonnes						
ratio 10^9 bricks : 10^6 t cement						

This confirms the suggestion that bricks have lost market share to concrete during the period 1960 to 1990. In fact, Figure 39 does not tell the full story, because whereas there were only about half a million tonnes of cement a year imported into UK before the 1980s, that figure had risen to over 2 million tonnes in 1990, as cement became a more actively traded international commodity. On the other hand, the UK still produces the bulk of its own bricks.

It is interesting to compare the energy used in producing a similar weight of fired bricks and cement; could it be that the increasing cost of energy has helped to 'fuel' the move from bricks to cement? On average it takes about 200 kg of coal (or coal equivalent) to fire 1 000 bricks (each weighing about 2.5 kg) and about the same amount of fuel to produce a tonne of cement.

⬤ What are the comparative energy costs *per tonne* of bricks and cement?

⬤ Cement must consume 2 500/1 000 = 2.5 times as much energy per tonne as bricks.

It is clear that cement needs more energy than bricks per tonne of product. If cement is compared to bricks made from Oxford Clay (70 kg coal is burnt to make 1 000 bricks), then bricks are very much cheaper in energy terms than cement — almost seven times cheaper. (This is a good example of *energy accounting* mentioned in Block 1, as another way of evaluating competing materials.)

⬤ But why is this not a fair comparison of the costs of *building* a wall in these two materials?

⬤ (a)   Because bricks can only be laid if some cement is also used to make the mortar bonding. So a tonne of bricks cannot be used without some cement as well.

(b)   Cement is not used as a building material by itself, but for normal purposes is mixed with between 4 and 10 times its weight of cheaper aggregate and sand. So one tonne of cement produces many tonnes of finished building material. Generally, cement-based materials like concrete are cheaper than bricks, by the tonne of *finished* structure, and even cheaper if compared *per cubic metre*.

Table 14 gives some typical retail costs of building materials. Complete the final column (the readymix line has been done), and then try Question 21.

Table 14   Comparative costs of building materials (local retail prices, late 1992)

Material	Cost	Cost/£ per t	Density/t m^{-3}	Cost/£ per m^3
common bricks	£15 per 100	65	1.7	
facing bricks	£20 per 100	86	1.75	
hand-made bricks	£45 per 100	193	1.8	
cement blocks (= 6 bricks*)	£42 per 100	33	1.3	
lightweight blocks† (= 6 bricks*)	£65 per 100	135	0.5	
aggregate or sand	—	20	2	
cement	£3.60 for 50 kg	72	not relevant	not relevant
readymix concrete	—	24	2	48

* Cement and insulating blocks occupy the same volume in a wall as 6 bricks.

† Low-density blocks used for their good insulating properties.

Question 21

(a) Of the materials listed in Table 14, which is the cheapest by volume for building a small wall?

(b) Would this be the most *cost-effective* material for the inner skin of a house wall. If not, suggest which material(s) you would consider as an alternative?

The amount of limestone used in cement production is less than 25% of the limestone quarried in the UK, but there is no realistic prospect of the raw materials for cement production being in short supply, especially as cement is a relatively high value limestone product. On the other hand, with the increasing shipment of cargoes round the world in bulk carriers, there is probably a much greater threat to UK cement production from cheap imports than from shortages of supply at home.

5.3 Other uses of limestone

Limestone has a great many other uses, besides building stones, like Portland or Bath stone, and as a raw material for the cement industry.

You may have noticed that old walls used a different type of mortar from modern cement. It is much softer, and often much lighter coloured, almost white in some cases. This lime mortar was all that was available before cement was re-invented, and its use in stone buildings was standard even for much of the nineteenth century. Some argue that one reason why older buildings seem to 'bear their age with grace' is that lime mortar, being much less rigid than the stone, enables a building to 'give' a little, by allowing small movements in the soft mortar layers, which prevents major cracks developing through the stone or bricks.

Lime mortar is also made from limestone, by first heating the limestone, which drives off CO_2, leaving calcium oxide, CaO:

$$CaCO_3 = CaO + CO_2 \qquad (5.2)$$

Calcium oxide (sometimes called 'quicklime'), readily combines with water:

$$CaO + H_2O = Ca(OH)_2 \qquad (5.3)$$

The material produced here, calcium hydroxide, $Ca(OH)_2$ (sometimes called 'slaked lime'), is then mixed with sand to make lime mortar, which can be used like cement mortar.

Lime is also widely used in other industries. For example, CaO is a vital part of the iron and steel industry, where it is used in furnaces to make the slag used to remove impurities from the molten metal (recall Video Band 1).

$Ca(OH)_2$ has also been used for centuries to improve the agricultural properties of naturally acid soils. Small lime kilns, where locally quarried limestone was heated ('roasted') to make quicklime, can still be seen in limestone areas all over the country (Figure 40).

Powdered limestone itself is an important material: it too is spread on the land to improve the soil, and it is a major component of many powders, pastes, paint and fillers in plastics. 'Putty' used for fixing glass in windows is linseed oil mixed with powdered limestone, and some toothpaste contains a lot of powdered limestone.

Figure 40 Old limekiln. Local limestone was loaded in the top from the nearby quarry. A fire was started below, and the limestone heated to form CaO.

5.4 Summary of Section 5

1 Limestone is plentiful in Britain, and there is a wide variety of limestone which is exploited for different purposes. Limestone is widely used for building stones.

2 Limestone is an essential ingredient of cement, and hence of concrete, which has become the most important modern building material. It is used in a variety of cement-bound building blocks, which have been substituted for bricks in many uses.

3 Some pure limestones are almost pure calcium carbonate, and so can be worked for the production of chemicals such as calcium oxide, CaO, and calcium hydroxide, $Ca(OH)_2$.

6 EVAPORITES AND GYPSUM

6.1 Formation of evaporites

Seawater contains dissolved quantities of most elements, many originally derived from the weathering of crustal rocks, especially the more soluble metal ions, which have gone into solution as a result of chemical weathering of minerals like feldspars (Section 4.1, Figure 23). The concentration of these ions in river water is very low, often less than 120 parts per million (ppm) in total, but over geological time vast amounts of these materials have been carried from the land to the sea by the world's rivers. Much of the carbonate, chloride, bromide, etc., in seawater is derived from volcanic gases. Table 15 lists the constituents of seawater which are present in concentrations of more than 1 ppm. Because of the amount of water in the oceans, elements present in minute concentrations in seawater can still add up to huge quantities. However, sodium, chlorine, magnesium and bromine are the only elements to be extracted commercially from the oceans today.

Table 15 The abundance of dissolved elements in seawater, and the salts precipitated on evaporation

Element	Concentration/ ppm*	Salt formed on evaporation	% by weight of salt formed on total evaporation
chlorine, Cl	19 000	NaCl	78.04
sodium, Na	10 500	$MgCl_2$	9.21
magnesium, Mg	1 350	$MgSO_4$	6.53
sulphur, S	2 650	$CaSO_4.2H_2O$	3.48
calcium, Ca	400	$CaCO_3$	0.33
potassium, K	380	KCl	2.11
bromine, Br	65	$MgBr_2$	0.25
carbon, C	140		
strontium, Sr	8		
boron, B	4.6		
silicon, Si	3		
fluorine, F	1.3		
total dissolved salts	35 000†		

* ppm (parts per million) ≡ mg per litre.

† Total dissolved salts in seawater = 35 g per litre, or 3.5% by weight.

Magnesium is a very interesting example. Although it is present in seawater at a concentration of about 0.1% by weight, which is only about a hundredth of its concentration in common rocks like dolomite (a calcium–magnesium carbonate rock), it is cheaper to convert it into a useful form from seawater than from this rock. The reason is that it is relatively easy to precipitate magnesium hydroxide, $Mg(OH)_2$, by adding slaked lime, $Ca(OH)_2$, to seawater. $Mg(OH)_2$ is readily converted to magnesium oxide, MgO, which is used, for example, in refractory bricks to line steel furnaces. This acccounts for much of the industrial use of magnesium, so there is little need for the energy-intensive conversion to magnesium metal.

Where evaporation of seawater is greater than the inflow of fresh water from rivers, the dissolved elements become steadily more concentrated until the least-soluble salts reach saturation and are precipitated. Precipitation occurs not in order of the *abundances* of the dissolved materials, but in order of *least solubility*; that is, the least-soluble salts precipitate first. This sequence is shown in Figure 41. The percentage figures show the amount of the original seawater left at the point when each salt starts to precipitate; the relative proportions of salts formed are indicated by the sizes of the triangles below. The first compound to precipitate is calcium carbonate ($CaCO_3$), and this is the only material to form until evaporation has reduced the seawater to 19% of its original volume. This precipitate would form a limestone, such as the oolite in the Rock Kit.

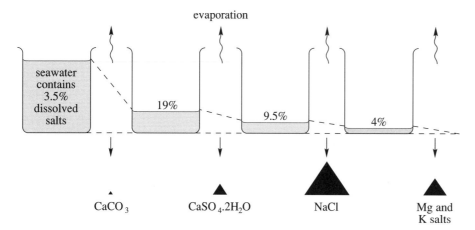

Figure 41   The succession of salts precipitated from seawater on evaporation. During evaporation of the first 81% of water, only $CaCO_3$ is formed. When evaporation has reduced the water volume to 19%, $CaSO_4.2H_2O$ starts to precipitate. When only 9.5% of the original water is left, NaCl begins to precipitate, and magnesium and potassium salts begin to come out of solution at 4% of the original volume. The sizes of the triangles indicate the relative proportions of the salts formed (see fourth column of Table 15).

When 81% of the seawater has evaporated, gypsum, $CaSO_4.2H_2O$, the first evaporite mineral, begins to form. In the crystal structure of gypsum, two molecules of water are associated with one calcium ion and one sulphate ion. Only if evaporation continues to less than 10% of the original water volume is it joined by the next least soluble mineral, halite (common salt), NaCl. But if evaporation proceeds beyond this point, huge quantities of NaCl can be obtained. The most soluble salts of all are the chlorides of potassium and magnesium; only when evaporation is almost complete are these salts thrown out of solution. In nature, complete evaporation to dryness of whole seas is very rare, and so these most soluble evaporite salts are rarely found preserved in sequences of sedimentary rocks.

Today, evaporite minerals are forming in shallow seas within 35° latitude of the Equator, but only in small amounts. However, in the geological record we can find evaporite mineral deposits which in total are tens or even hundreds of metres in thickness, as for example in the Permian strata (250 Ma) of north-east England and beneath the North Sea, and in Triassic rocks (200 Ma) in Cheshire, which contain the famous Cheshire salt beds.

Question 22

If a closed sea, 100 m deep, evaporated completely, what thickness, in metres, of the following evaporite minerals would be formed (assume each mineral has an average density of about $2\,000\,kg\,m^{-3}$)?

(a) NaCl;

(b) gypsum.

It is clear from the above that the formation of layers of evaporite mineral deposits, hundreds of metres thick, required the evaporation of vast quantities of seawater. We believe that this can occur only in shallow water where the Sun heats up the water to cause fast evaporation. In addition two further conditions must be met:

(a) subsidence of the sea floor on which they are forming, or the salts would just build up to sea-level, and

(b) frequent replenishment of the seawater.

A typical situation might be a bay or arm of the sea, partly cut off from the open sea by a submerged barrier, giving a shallow shelf through which ocean water can replenish water lost by evaporation. For most of the time only the least-soluble salts, gypsum and halite, would form, and only if the sea almost completely dried up would the most soluble potassium and magnesium salts precipitate.

Figure 42 shows two sequences of evaporite minerals actually found in the geological record, and a blank column for use with Question 23.

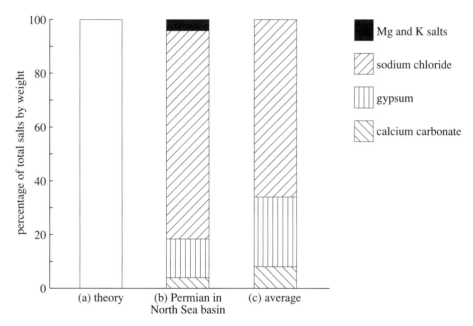

Figure 42 Relative abundances of the major evaporite minerals: (a) theoretical abundances for Question 23; (b) average of Permian sequences beneath the North Sea; (c) average of all evaporite sequences in the geological record.

Question 23

Figure 42 shows the sequences of evaporites found in the North Sea (b); and an average for all the world's evaporites (c).

(i) Fill in column (a) in Figure 42 to show the proportions of evaporite minerals which would be expected theoretically if complete evaporation of typical seawater occurred today (Table 15).

(ii) Which evaporite mineral is more abundant in evaporites found in nature (columns in Figure 42b and c), compared with the theoretical abundance to be expected from complete seawater evaporation (Figure 42a), and why might this be so?

(iii) Which evaporite minerals are less abundant in evaporites (Figure 42b and c), compared with the theoretical column, (a), and why might this be so?

6.2 Gypsum, plaster of Paris, and plasterboard

Gypsum, $CaSO_4.2H_2O$, is a soft, white mineral, which is a form of calcium sulphate. It usually occurs in layers in soft sediments, from where it can be easily extracted either in open-cast excavations, or in shallow mines. It is often found associated with the related mineral, anhydrite, $CaSO_4$. The chief use for gypsum is in the manufacture of gypsum plaster and plasterboard, although it is also used as a component of cement, to slow down the rate of setting.

In the UK a typical house has internal walls covered with a thin layer of gypsum plaster (about 3 mm), to give a smooth finish, and usually ceilings consist of sheets of plasterboard (about 8 mm) attached to the bottom of the joists. This means that a typical three-bedroom house can contain between one and three tonnes of gypsum. How does gypsum from the ground become plaster or plasterboard in the house?

Look at the following equation:

$$2CaSO_4.2H_2O \rightleftharpoons 2CaSO_4.\tfrac{1}{2}H_2O + 3H_2O \qquad\qquad (6.1)$$
$$\text{gypsum} \qquad\qquad \text{hemihydrate}$$

The forward reaction in Equation 6.1 is a dehydration reaction, in which heat expels all but a half of the two molecules of water from gypsum to form hemihydrate, whose formula includes only half a water molecule. Hemihydrate is the main constituent of plaster of Paris, made by heating gypsum. It is the material used both for plastering walls, and for soaking bandages to make casts for broken limbs. When plaster of Paris (hemihydrate) is mixed with water, rehydration occurs to produce the dihydrate, gypsum (the reverse reaction in Equation 6.1).

This is a good example of a **reversible chemical reaction**. In this case, heat *dehydrates* (drives water off) the gypsum to give plaster of Paris, which can then be *rehydrated* (water added) by mixing with water at low temperature.

You may be interested to know that gypsum is a very important material in fire protection in buildings: can you think why? When a room is on fire, the door is usually the most vulnerable part of the structure. Fire doors are often made incorporating a thick layer of gypsum plasterboard. The gypsum provides good fire resistance because the water held in the gypsum has to be 'boiled off' by the heat of the fire before the flame can break through the door. Similarly, a plasterboard ceiling provides a considerable check to the spread of fire, and firebreaks in lofts are often made of plasterboard.

You may like to simulate the preparation of plaster of Paris for yourself, starting with the gypsum sample in the Rock Kit, and then try the following question.

Activity 5 From gypsum to plaster of Paris to gypsum

The small piece of white gypsum in the Rock Kit is much softer than all the other samples. The mineral is white if pure; most samples are formed of long shiny crystals, hence the name 'satin spar' (samples may be slightly coloured by the reddish brown mud in which the gypsum is found).

Put it in a moderate oven for about half an hour on a piece of aluminium foil (this is done industrially, at about 170 °C for 1–3 hours). It should now be plaster of Paris. Take it out; you should be able to easily powder it between a couple of spoons or pieces of wood. If this powder is mixed to a stiff paste with a little water, it is ready for use as plaster and if left for 15 minutes or so, it will set hard.

If you put the plaster sample back in the oven, dehydration will occur again to re-form the plaster of Paris, which in turn can be mixed with water as before to re-form gypsum, as indicated in Equation 6.1. This process can be repeated as many times as you wish.

You can also make your own 'plasterboard' if the wet plaster of Paris is put into a roll of absorbent paper and gently flattened. As the crystals of gypsum grow on setting, they penetrate into the paper to bind the two together.

Question 24

How does this reversible reaction differ from the reaction with water used to cement grains in the sugar together in Section 2.1.5? In both cases, water seems to cause cementation.

Each year large quantities of gypsum are produced world wide (about 100 million tonnes in 1990), chiefly for plaster and plasterboard manufacture. In the UK about 4 million tonnes are mined each year; in 1990 a further 0.6 million tonnes were imported. Total EU production is about 16 million tonnes. Desulphurization of power station flue gases is now becoming an important source of gypsum. Sulphur dioxide is removed from the flue gases by combination with limestone:

$$2CaCO_3 + 2SO_2 + O_2 + 4H_2O = 2CaSO_4.2H_2O + 2CO_2 \qquad (6.2)$$

Up to 1 million tonnes of gypsum a year are being produced by a single power station at Drax in Yorkshire.

6.3 Summary of Section 6

1   When seawater evaporates in a closed basin, evaporite minerals are formed, in the following sequence of increasing solubility: calcite, gypsum, halite, followed by soluble potassium and magnesium salts.

2   Gypsum, $CaSO_4.2H_2O$, is widely used for the manufacture of plaster, plasterboard and plaster of Paris.

3   Gypsum changes to plaster of Paris in a reversible chemical reaction involving the loss of water.

7 CRUSHED ROCK AGGREGATES

Section 3 discussed sands and gravels, materials that were chiefly laid down since the last glacial period on top of the solid rocks shown on the *Postcard Geological Map*. These sands and gravels are the traditional and cheapest source of aggregates for the building industry in most of the UK.

⬤ What is the principal source of aggregate in the UK today: sand and gravel, recycled wastes or crushed rock (Section 3.1)? Is there any recent trend in aggregate production?

⬤ Before the 1970s, sand and gravel dominated the supply, but today we are using more and more crushed rock instead of sand and gravel (Figure 15). Recycled wastes account for only a small percentage of the total aggregate supply.

Question 25

What possible reasons could account for the move away from traditional sand and gravel resources towards aggregates made from crushed rocks in recent years?

Quarries worked for crushed-rock aggregates are subject to more stringent planning permission and working conditions than sand and gravel pits because there is inevitably more disturbance in the immediate vicinity. For example, the rock has to be blasted from the quarry face and then crushed before being screened to final sizes, so, in general, crushed-rock quarries tend to be noisier and dustier than sand and gravel pits. The crushed-rock quarries are also much larger, because the more complicated method of working involves considerable capital investment. A high output of aggregate is therefore needed to make the operation economic. Some hard-rock aggregate quarries are very big indeed, with outputs of several million tonnes a year.

For some modern construction projects, especially roads and high-strength concretes, crushed-rock aggregate is a more suitable material than sand and gravel. There are other specialized applications like the ballast below railway tracks, where high crushing strength is needed, and here crushed-rock aggregates have always been preferred. Most railway ballast is made from igneous or metamorphic rock in the UK, but the market for railway ballast is modest today — only 3 to 4 million tonnes a year.

7.1 Sedimentary rocks as aggregates

Conditions for establishing an aggregate quarry in a sedimentary rock include:

- The rock must be strong, and of low porosity, so it is not easily frost damaged: this normally means a well-cemented rock.
- The site should contain a large quantity of the rock; this means the bed of rock needs to be thick and of constant physical properties.
- The rock should be readily accessible beneath a shallow overburden; this often means that the layers of sedimentary rock should be horizontal or nearly so.
- The site should ideally be able to be worked without flooding, and be somewhere suitable for quarrying, crushing and transporting the stone; this means a site above the water table, or one easily pumped dry.

- The site should not be too close to a town so that the quarrying does not present a nuisance, but should be reasonably close to markets to minimize transport costs.

⬤ Will a large quarry producing crushed sedimentary rock aggregate tend to have a lower or higher place value than a small sand and gravel pit?

⬤ It will depend on the market that is being supplied, which in turn will be determined by the quality of the aggregate itself. Unless the aggregate has special qualities which open up markets not available to sand and gravel, both will have a high place value, and so only a very local distribution.

The sedimentary rocks that best fit these criteria are the better-cemented sandstones and limestones, which tend to be those older than Permian (280 Ma). As you can see from the *Postcard Geological Map*, these Carboniferous and older rocks generally occur to the north and west of a Torquay–Humber–Newcastle upon Tyne line, especially Devon and Cornwall, South Wales, the Pennines and the central valley of Scotland. By far the most widely quarried rock is the Carboniferous Limestone, because it has low porosity, is strong and uniform in its properties, and is widely available in thick beds close to urban centres. Some Carboniferous sandstones are used for aggregate, but generally most sandstones in the UK are too porous and not well-enough cemented, and so are liable to frost damage. Some Jurassic limestones are used, but tend to be thinner, more porous, and much softer than the Carboniferous ones.

Porosity and frost damage

Rocks and other porous materials can suffer from frost damage if they are used in buildings where they can become soaked with water and then frozen. This is especially true of permeable rocks, which can absorb a lot of water, and those in which the mineral grains are poorly cemented. When water in the pores of a rock turns to ice, it expands. This can cause the rock to split, and in extreme cases it is turned to a crumbling mass of fragments.

A qualitative method to test porosity is to half immerse a rock in water: porous and permeable materials allow water to be drawn up well above the water level in which they are standing, like the oil in the wick of an old lamp.

The porosity of building materials can easily be measured with simple scales. Firstly, the sample should be heated to drive off any water already present in the pores, and weighed. Then it is totally immersed in water for about 20 minutes, the surface quickly dried off, and the sample reweighed. (Air coming out of any pores appears as bubbles on the surface of an immersed rock or brick, the size of the bubbles being some indication of the pore sizes: a stream of bubbles usually indicates a crack.) The weight gain is the amount of water absorbed into the pores, so from the difference between the 'dry' and 'wet' weights, the porosity can be calculated. Table 16 shows results on everyday materials, using simple scales, and drying samples in a domestic oven.

After allowing for the difference in density between water ($1\,\mathrm{t\,m^{-3}}$) and the various building materials (usually about $2\,\mathrm{t\,m^{-3}}$), the porosity is easily calculated. From Section 2.2.2, we know that porosity is defined as the percentage volume of the pores in the rock (vol. water/vol. rock × 100%).

So porosity =

$$\frac{\text{wt of water absorbed}}{\text{wt of dry material / dry density}} \times 100\%$$

Therefore, in Table 16, the porosity in the bottom row is calculated as follows:

$$\frac{\text{row c}}{\text{row a / row e}} \times 100\%$$

Question 26

(a)   You are provided with the weights of a series of building materials, including two limestones A and B, weighed wet and dry. Calculate their porosity by completing Table 16.

(b)   Which material has the lowest and which the highest porosity?

(c)   Which of the two limestones is likely to show the better resistance to frost shattering when used in an exposed garden wall?

Table 16 Building materials weighed wet and dry to estimate porosity

	Engineering brick	Common brick	FBA* cement block	Lightweight block†	Concrete	Limestone A	Limestone B
(a) dry wt/kg	3.45	2.34	0.30	0.385	0.600	1.10	1.31
(b) wt after water immersion for 20 min./kg	3.45	2.53	0.325	0.40	0.605	1.14	1.30
(c) gain in wt/kg	0	0.19	0.025	0.015	0.005	0.04	0.01
(d) gain in wt/%	0	8.1	8.3	3.9	0.8	3.5	0.8
(e) density/t m^{-3}	2.0	1.7	1.3	0.5	2.0	2.6	2.6
(f) porosity/% of dry volume‡					1.7		

* FBA: furnace bottom ash; cement block made from the clinker removed from power station furnaces.

† Low-density block used for its good insulating properties.

‡ True porosity after allowing for the varying densities of the different materials (row e). The denser the material involved, the more the porosity increases.

7.2 Igneous and metamorphic rocks as aggregates

Igneous and metamorphic rocks in general make excellent aggregates because they are tough materials with strong interlocking textures and very low porosity. Most igneous rocks make good aggregates, but many metamorphic rocks such as slates and schists have a strong preferred alignment of their minerals, causing them to split into long, platey fragments, which cannot be easily consolidated to form a compact low-porosity aggregate. Some igneous and metamorphic rocks contain very large crystals. For example, the pink feldspars in the granite in the Rock Kit can be 2 cm or more in length. If such large crystals have well-developed cleavage planes (as feldspars and micas do), then any aggregate fragment of a similar size to these large crystals will be weakened by these cleavage planes and liable to split.

Looking at the *Postcard Geological Map*, it is clear than most of the igneous and metamorphic rocks occur in western and northern parts of the country, far away from the main aggregate market in south-east England. To meet the demand for high-quality aggregates in the south-east, transport over long distances is required.

7.3 Aggregates for concrete

It is hard to believe that the widespread use of concrete as a replacement for stone and brick has largely occurred in the last 70 years (Figure 14, Section 3.1), while the use of structural beams made of concrete reinforced with steel rods has become common even more recently, and replaced many all-steel

(a)

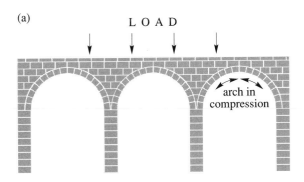

(b)

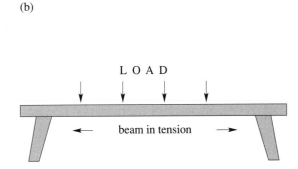

structures such as girder bridges. The combination of steel and concrete makes it possible to use concrete in entirely new ways from all other materials discussed so far in this Block (Figure 43).

⬤ What crucial property does steel give to concrete which is responsible for this difference?

⬤ Steel enables concrete to resist pulling forces, which cause *tensile stresses* in the structures. This allows the construction of long concrete beams, which can be used to span distances, without the use of arches.

Figure 43 (a) Masonry (stone or brick); (b) steel or reinforced-concrete bridges. In (a) the load is supported by the material in the arches being compressed; in (b) the load is carried by the resistance of the beam in tension.

This also means that a bridge made of steel or reinforced-concrete beams can sustain large loads using much less material than a masonry bridge built of brick or natural stone. These two latter materials are strong in compression, but very weak in tension, which is why you never see a natural stone lintel more than a metre or so in length.

The aim of concrete-making is to produce a hard stable material, which develops a high strength as the cement sets. This is best achieved when all the aggregate particles are coated with cement and stuck together, and there is the minimum of pore space between the aggregate fragments. Since much of the water added to concrete forms small pores, the least amount of water possible is always used in concrete, in order to maximize final strength.

Most rocks with a high crushing strength will make good aggregate, but the strongest concrete is made with the correct shape, size and grading of aggregate. The best concrete is made from aggregate that meets the following requirements:

1 *Shape* Fragments should be equidimensional — more or less equal in size in all directions, but still irregular in shape — rather than flat, spherical or elongated. Crushed slate makes a particularly poor high-porosity aggregate.

2 *Size* In general, coarse aggregates (above 40 mm) are only used when large masses of concrete more than a metre thick are being cast; if there are large aggregate fragments in concrete depths of less than a metre, it is difficult to be sure that all air pockets have been eliminated.

3 *Grading* It is vital that there is a mixture of sizes, so that smaller particles fill all the spaces between the larger ones, leaving as little unfilled pore space as possible. This also ensures the maximum aggregate-to-aggregate contact, which gives the concrete its strength (Figure 4b and d). An ideal aggregate is one in which the particles form a cumulative frequency curve which is almost a straight line with a shallow slope (as in Figure 4f). In practice, much of the blending of aggregate sizes is done by 'rule of thumb' to give a good dense aggregate mix on the basis of experience of the particular rock being used.

Specifications for concrete aggregate tend to be written in terms of a **grading envelope**, which specifies the maximum and minimum limits of the cumulative frequency curves within which the mixture of aggregate sizes should fall (Figure 44).

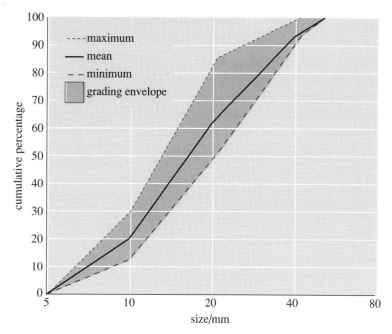

Figure 44 Particle size distribution curves for an aggregate, showing how permissible limits are defined by the maximum and minimum cumulative frequency curves to give a grading envelope (compare Figure 4b and f, but note that here the size increases to the right). The *steeper* the curve, the smaller the range of particle sizes; the *narrower* the grading envelope, the more precisely the aggregate size ranges are specified.

Aggregates are tested by sieving a sample into the different sizes and then plotting the weight of each size fraction as a histogram, or a cumulative frequency curve, to check that the results fall inside the grading envelope for the job in hand. The top and bottom of the grading envelope specify the sizes of the smallest and largest particles to be used.

○ What term is used differently by geologists and engineers to describe the grading of particle sizes shown in curves like those in Figure 44 (Section 3.1)?

○ Sorting. To a geologist, such a mixture occurring in a sediment would be a *poorly sorted* material; to an engineer it is a well-graded mixture ready for use, and so is called *well sorted*.

○ Is the mixture in Figure 44 a coarse-grained or fine-grained aggregate?

○ With the range of sizes running from 5 to 50 mm, it is a coarse-grained one (Figure 13).

4   *Surface texture*   Cement will stick to most rocks. Indeed, for many purposes, even smooth flint pebbles make perfectly satisfactory concrete aggregates, but a rough surface texture makes the best bond to cement. Fine particles such as clay minerals or dust from crushing have to be kept to a minimum (less than 5%), since they tend to coat the aggregate particles, and so prevent the cement from sticking.

5   *Physical suitability*   Fragments of unsuitable materials must be excluded, such as high-porosity rock (which is susceptible to frost damage) and weak, easily crushed material.

6   *Chemical suitability*   Aggregate must not contain reactive chemicals. It is vital to remove all the salt from marine gravels, since the presence of sodium chloride can lead to damaging reactions with cement in damp conditions. Common sulphide minerals, such as iron pyrites, FeS_2, can

also cause problems by reacting with the cement. Some rocks react chemically with the highly alkaline solutions formed when cement sets. It has been found that some volcanic rocks contain a glassy type of silica which reacts with these solutions to form compounds that can exert an internal pressure on the concrete as high as $14\,\text{MN}\,\text{m}^{-2}$, causing cracking.

Concrete used in foundations must be stable when soaked by the water present in the ground. In areas where groundwater is rich in sulphate, sulphate-resistant cement, SRC (which has a higher iron content than OPC), has to be used. Similarly, concrete used in reinforced and pre-stressed beams and panels must not contain material that will react with either the steel in the reinforcing rods, or with the industrial atmosphere in which it is to be used.

In this country, most concrete comes from 'readymix' plants providing a delivery service to a local area. They are usually limited to a radius of about 20–30 km, because once water has been added to cement the concrete must be poured within 2 hours. As much as possible of the aggregate will be from local sources, so concrete aggregate quarries are needed all over the country, especially near the main population centres where demand is greatest. Concrete for special purposes, commanding a higher price, may use higher-quality aggregates from more remote sources.

Question 27

Which two samples in the Rock Kit would be least suitable as an aggregate for high-strength concrete, and why?

Activity 6

Do you know where the aggregate used in your local concrete comes from, whether it is from sands and gravels or crushed rock, and what are the main rock types it contains?

Comment A visit to your local builders' merchants or 'readymix' concrete plant should soon settle it. In the area around Milton Keynes, I found that the sand and gravel used was from local river valley sand and gravel deposits. The larger particles in the gravel were chiefly flint, with some fragments of the local Jurassic limestone. For higher-quality concrete, aggregates from further north were used, either gravels from the Trent valley, which contained a high proportion of quartz pebbles, or crushed igneous rock from Charnwood in Leicestershire (Plate 23).

7.4 Aggregates for roads

● How much of the aggregate used in the UK goes into roads (10%, 30%, 50% or 70%), and how much is needed for one kilometre of new motorway?

● Just over 30%, and up to 100 000 t (Tables 6 and 7).

These two figures highlight just how important the demand for aggregates from road-building has become; more aggregate is being used for roads than for anything else. In a small highly populated industrialized country like the UK, this demand is most keenly felt because we have a high concentration of people, and therefore roads, in a small area. The world average density of paved road is just less than 100 km per 1 000 km². In North America it is about twice as high; in the EU as a whole about ×8, and in the UK about ×16. In the south-east of England it is about four times as high as the average for the UK as a whole — in other words about 30 times as high as the average for North America. This sets the scene for probably the biggest environmental issue related to building materials in the UK today. Not only are huge volumes of aggregate needed to build the roads, but also both the roads themselves and the aggregate quarries take up scarce land in the most densely populated area of the country, where other demands for land are very high.

7.4.1 History of roads

What is a road? This may seem a trivial question, but there is a huge variety of roads in different places in the world today, which are very different from ancient roads. In simplest terms a road is a route to enable people and goods to travel from one place to another, and is built to suit local traffic and conditions, from materials which are readily available.

Across a desert with few people and sparse traffic, the main priority is to mark the route, and little preparation of the road surface is needed. The biggest hazard is getting lost when it is possible to drive for hundreds of miles in any direction without seeing a settlement. Through tropical rain-forest, where again traffic is often light, trees may need felling, and the main surface preparation is drainage to keep the road open in the wet season. In industrialized countries today, paved roads for modern vehicles need a smooth, hard-wearing surface, with shallow gradients for comfort, speed and good fuel consumption.

In Roman times, when roads were built for dispatching armies across the empire as quickly as possible, straight roads were the priority, the road surface was less important, and steep gradients were not limitations for marching soldiers. In heavily used streets in towns the Romans laid large slabs of stone, ideal for both marching feet and horse-drawn carts, and there are still examples of Roman stone 'pavements' in good repair after nearly 2 000 years of use. Many Roman roads were carefully made with several layers of compacted broken stone of different sizes, not unlike present-day roads.

Up to the eighteenth century, roads in this country were notorious for their poor surfaces, which feature in tales of highwaymen and stagecoaches stuck in the mud. The distances between towns were too long for all roads to be surfaced with slabs of dressed stone, and carriage wheels inevitably made huge ruts in the surface of wet and muddy roads.

The main advance towards the modern method of long-distance road construction was made in the late eighteenth century by John McAdam, a lowland Scot, who was the first to systematically use crushed stone of different sizes, so that smaller stones filled up the holes between larger ones to form a smooth compacted 'pavement' — a method which bears his name to this day. No cement or binder was used by McAdam, the strength of the road coming merely from the well-graded nature of the broken stone fragments (none of which was larger than a hen's egg) which were further compacted by the wheels of the traffic. Compaction gave his road surfaces a low porosity. In addition he raised the centre of the road above the edges to throw water off both sides of the road, so the ground below a McAdam road stayed *dry* — the crucial improvement for preserving the road in wet weather.

McAdam was a stickler for detail, as can be seen from the following extracts from his book, *Remarks on the Present System of Roadmaking*, 7th edn, 1823.

On preparing aggregate for a 'McAdam' road:

The only proper method of breaking stones, both for effect and economy, is by persons *sitting*; the stones are to be placed in small heaps, and women, boys, or old men past hard labour, must sit down with small hammers and break them, so as none shall exceed six ounces in weight. (p. 40)

On the materials to be used:

Every road is to be made of broken stone without mixture of earth, clay, chalk, or any other matter that will imbibe water, and be affected with frost; nothing is to be laid on the clean stone on pretence of *binding*; broken stone will combine by its own angles into a smooth solid surface that cannot be affected by the vicissitudes of the weather, or displaced by the action of wheels, which pass over it without a jolt, and consequently without injury. (p. 40)

On the importance of dry road foundations:

As no artificial road can ever be made so good, and so useful as the natural soil in a *dry state*, it is only necessary to procure, and preserve this dry state of so much ground as is intended to be occupied by a road. (p. 41)

The first operation in making a road should be the reverse of digging a trench. The road should not be sunk below, but rather raised above, the ordinary level of the adjacent ground, care should at any rate be taken, that there be a sufficient fall to take off water, so that it should always be some inches below the level of the ground upon which the road is intended to be placed: this must be done, either by making drains to lower ground, or if that be not practicable, from the nature of the country, then the soil upon which the road is proposed to be laid, must be raised by addition, so as to be some inches above the level of the water. (p. 50)

On the importance of keeping out rainwater:

The thickness of such a road is immaterial, as to its strength for carrying weight; this object is already obtained by providing a dry surface, over which the road is to be placed as a covering, or roof, to preserve it in that state: experience having shewn, that if water passes through a road, and fill the native soil, the road, whatever may be its thickness, loses its support, and goes to pieces. (p. 51)

In McAdam's day, roads were built and maintained on the revenue from tolls, leading to a keen awareness of prices:

The price of lifting a rough road, breaking the stones, forming the road, smoothing the surface, cleaning out the water courses, and replacing the stone, leaving the road in a finished state, has been found in practice to be from one penny to two pence per superficial yard, lifted four inches deep; the variation of price depends on the greater of lesser quantity of stone to be broken. At two pence per yard a road of six yards wide will cost, therefore, one shilling per running yard, or 88l. [£88] per mile. (p. 41) and of traffic costs:

> Waggons and carts with wheels of a cylindrical form and upright bearing,
> running on a breadth of tire of five and six inches, cannot injure a well
> made road, at the slow pace with which such carriages travel; at least,
> in any proportion beyond the toll they pay. On the contrary, it is certain,
> that Stage Coaches, with their present system of loading, and velocity of
> travelling upon very narrow wheeels, damage the roads in a much greater
> proportion than the compensation derived from the toll. (p. 14)

As a practical man, McAdam was well aware that it was vital for the toll road
Trustees to appoint the right staff to be in charge of road construction, at a time
before highway engineering was an established profession:

> This very dangerous error consists in employing persons who offer
> themselves as having been instructed in Road making on scientific
> principles, without due inquiry respecting their skill, industry, and moral
> character. Among the persons who present themselves to be instructed, a
> very small proportion acquire a competent knowledge of their profession,
> and this number is farther diminished by subsequent dismission for
> negligence, drunkenness, and dishonesty. Of these rejected and incapable
> persons, great numbers are spread over the Country, soliciting employ-
> ment; and many have been incautiously engaged by Trustees, without
> inquiry either as to their character or their ability in their profession. (p. ii)

In Victorian times, city streets were needed to carry the heavy traffic for the
new industries, and these were largely paved with blocks of stone. Cubes of
stone 'sets' or 'cobblestones' formed the road surface, because their uneven
broken surfaces and the gaps between provided a good grip for the edges of
the horses' shoes. This was important because all the driving power, and much
of the braking power too, came from the friction between the horseshoe and the
road; no power was obtained through the wheels, although they could be used
for braking.

Steel-rimmed cartwheels (narrow to minimize friction) subjected the road
surface to high pressures, and would quickly grind away soft rocks, so crystalline metamorphic and igneous rocks were often used for cobblestones. This
must have been expensive, but a layer of 15 cm cobbles would last for many
years, and many were in use for 100 years or more; as far as the Victorian
quarry owners were concerned, these city streets were indeed 'paved with
gold.' Similar high crushing-strength stone was also needed for kerbstones to
withstand the scuffing of steel wheels, and the demand for these tough stones
led to the shipping of igneous and metamorphic rocks, such as the Erquy Red
Beds quartzite, and Aberdeen and Cornish granites, to major centres of population such as London, Bristol and Cardiff.

Cobbled roads had a base of crushed rock to spread the load onto the soil
below, since the wheel of a heavy cart would soon displace cobblestones lying
directly on soil, especially if the soil was wet. To prevent this, the road was
waterproofed, the cobbles were often set in tar (hence the name 'set' for such
cobbles) as in Plate 24a, and drains laid to carry rainwater away. All good
roads in wet climates need to be waterproof, because if the soil below a road
becomes wet, it will soon collapse.

Alongside the cobbled streets, Victorian pavements were also largely made of
stone, chiefly medium to fine-grained sandstones (**flagstones**) which could be
easily split into thin sheets (flags) along bedding surfaces rich in mica flakes.
These flags were not so hardwearing as the igneous cobbles, but they provided
a high-friction surface for pedestrians' shoes.

Hard crystalline cobblestones may develop a polish under the wear of cartwheels, but the grip for the horses still came from the *macro-scale features* of the spaces between the stones, against which the horses' shoes could grip (Plate 24). But flagstones wear in a different way: they lose quartz grains which break out of the natural cement. The surface never polishes, and the sharp edges of the freshly exposed quartz grains always give a good grip for shoes because the sharp quartz grains provide a high-friction *micro-scale* surface. The best flagstones come from Elland in Yorkshire, of Carboniferous age (300 Ma), and are often called 'York stone'; they are still used for the best pavements. Many local authorities are re-laying natural stone kerbstones and flagstones after street refurbishment, an interesting example of the re-use of building materials.

York flagstones tend to have a higher permeability than modern concrete paving slabs, and so water drains away more easily, to give a better micro-friction grip in the wet. But many concrete paving slabs use the principle of macro-friction, by incorporating chippings of hard crystalline rock in the top surface. These tend to stand proud of the softer concrete slab.

The principle of micro-scale high friction is used on smooth stone or concrete stairs by sticking antislip strips of the black compound, silicon carbide, to the edges of the steps. Silicon carbide (also known as carborundum), SiC, is a widely used industrial abrasive, harder than quartz, and probably most familiar as the black 'wet-and-dry' abrasive paper used for rubbing down metalwork. It is also recommended for the abrasion tests in Activity 8.

In the typical Victorian cobbled street, all the principles of good road-building were fulfilled by the selection of building materials whose physical properties were matched to the different functions needed:

- firm basecourse to spread the load;
- waterproof surface and efficient drainage to prevent water penetration and softening of the road base;
- hard-wearing layer to resist the abrasion of steel traffic wheels, and a high-friction surface on a macro-scale to give the horseshoes a good grip, to facilitate propulsion and braking;
- large tough igneous kerbstones, which are difficult to break or dislodge even with heavy waggons on the kerb;
- micro-scale high-friction flagstones on the pavements, for pedestrian safety;
- ease of maintenance and repair; if the road or pavement had to be dug up, nearly all the original materials could be replaced afterwards; in resource terms this was very efficient, because the costly raw materials could be re-used directly.

Few of these Victorian cobble streets remain in the UK (an example is shown in Plate 24), though more have been left in inner cities in other EU countries, where the rumbling noise with modern traffic acts as an inbuilt traffic calming feature.

Question 28

(a) Of the samples in the Rock Kit, which one would you consider most promising for use in paving stones on a hill? Why might it not be entirely satisfactory?

(b) Which samples would you select as the best materials for kerbstones, and why?

Activity 7 Local paving and kerbstones

If your locality has any natural paving stones and kerbstones left, it is sometimes possible to find out what they are and where they came from.

In Northampton and Bedford, where I looked, there are many examples of large igneous kerbstones, with Shap and Cornish granite positively identifiable (Plate 14a and b). Modern concrete kerbs are easily recognized by their uniform size and shape, and lack of crystalline texture.

In these towns there are York stone flags, both old, worn ones, some of which have recently been relaid, and new, smooth, machine-sawn ones, with a distinctive natural swirling pattern of brown iron-staining.

Modern concrete paving stones can be recognized by their uniform sizes and appearance; the ones I saw used an igneous rock from the Charnwood area ('markfieldite', which has a distinctive pink and green speckled appearance) as aggregate, and some had a surface 'dressing' of 1 cm chips to give a macro-friction surface. All concrete products show small air bubbles on broken surfaces, and on one side still carry the patterned, dimpled surface of the mould. If you do find some York flags, you might see if you can tell any difference in friction between them and concrete paving slabs, especially when wet.

7.4.2 Modern high-speed roads

Before discussing the supply of aggregates used in the construction and repair of roads, which account for so much of the present aggregate demand, we shall consider how stone is used in modern roads. Modern road surfaces, which are still based on the principles laid down by McAdam, are of two types:

> a *rigid road* is made by casting a series of short slabs of concrete prepared from carefully graded stone particles and sand, bound with cement;

> a *flexible bitumen-bound* **macadam** *('tarmacadam') road*, is laid in long, smooth stretches, built up from a series of firmly consolidated layers of aggregate bound with bitumen*.

Both bitumen-bound and concrete road surfaces can be built on thick foundations to take heavy traffic, and in both cases the cardinal principles established for the Victorian road have to be followed.

⬤   What are the four most important features for a modern trunk road or motorway?

◗   (i)   Firm load-bearing base;
       (ii)   dry foundation;
       (iii)   hard-wearing, waterproof surface layer;
       (iv)   high-friction surface for braking and skid resistance.

Today, heavier axle loadings and much faster speeds mean that the roads have to be stronger (and therefore thicker), so more aggregates are needed. It is also probably true that since the road surface is today made of quite small rock particles artificially stuck together, it is likely to wear faster then the Victorian cobbled street made of solid blocks of granite.

---

* Bitumen is the highest-boiling fraction obtained from the distillation of crude oil.

7.4.3 Anatomy of a modern trunk road

Most bitumen-bound roads have four layers, which are sometimes referred to as the **road pavement**. Concrete roads generally have a single concrete layer instead of the three upper layers in Figure 45 and Plate 25a.

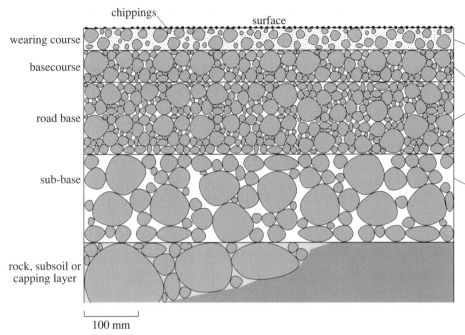

Figure 45 Sectional view through the four-layered structure of a modern tar-macadam road. The *wearing course* is made from fine-grained asphalt, with a high bitumen content, and skid-resistant chips rolled into its surface. The *basecourse* and *road base* are made from high crushing-strength bituminous macadam and well-graded (max. 40 mm) aggregate. They must be well compacted, since they act as the main load-distributing layers. The *sub-base* is the lower layer, and is made of large rock fragments only. It contains no binder, and its high porosity allows free drainage. It may be of variable thickness, and must have a level top surface.

Before the road itself can be laid, the ground must be levelled off to give the correct gradient for the road; shallow gradients are used wherever possible to ease traffic flow. The ground surface may be very soft and if so has to be covered with sand or broken rock to form a capping layer, which provides a starting point for the road proper. At this stage also the drainage is set out, and if necessary the capping layer is built up above the water level in the ground. Each layer is designed to carry out the different functions needed of the road:

*   **sub-base**: well drained with spaces to prevent water being drawn up into the road; there is no binder in the aggregate; it provides the level surface for the upper layers of the road;

*   **basecourse** and **road base**: coarse-grained, high crushing-strength aggregate in a dense bituminous macadam, compacted to less than 7% porosity for good load-bearing characteristics;

*   **wearing course**: waterproof, with skid-resistant chips rolled into its top to give high friction to the final road surface; it must not deform under braking conditions.

The details of materials used in these layers are shown in Table 17.

Table 17 Relative proportions of materials used in the top four layers of a modern tarmacadam road

	Thickness/mm	Max. size aggregate/mm	Aggregate	Sand	Filler/CaCO$_3$	Bitumen
wearing course (**asphalt**)	15–50	20	30%	52%	10%	8%
basecourse	50–80	40	95%	0	0	4.7%
road base	100–200	40	96%	0	0	3.5–4%
sub-base	250	75	100%	0	0	0
capping layer	300–500	125	local 'fill'	0	0	0

7.4.4 Resources for modern roads

Now would be a good time to watch the third part of Video Band 5: *Rocks for Roads*, starting about 15 minutes into the tape. This section deals with resources for a modern trunk road.

Video Band 5   Rocks for Roads

Speaker

Dean Welburn   Technical Manager RMC Roadstone

Dean Welburn describes how he supplies a local igneous rock for all the layers for 'dualling' the A1 in Northumberland. The quarry at Belford lies a few kilometres from the North Sea coast opposite the Farne Islands, shown as a single island on the *Postcard Geological Map*. The rock used is the Whin Sill, a sheet of intrusive basalt (strictly a dolerite, which has the same mineralogy, but is slightly coarser grained than a basalt), which is shown as the second isolated blob of red igneous rock crossed on the London to Edinburgh journey (Question 3, *Postcard Geological Map*). In fact the Whin Sill runs right across Northumberland and out to sea at the Farne Islands. In many places, Hadrian's Wall follows the outcrop of the Whin Sill (p. 19 of *The Geological Map* booklet).

For this road-widening scheme, once bulldozers have levelled the ground, a capping layer of sand and gravel from local temporary excavations is laid. All the other aggregate material for the road layers is prepared from the Whin Sill by blasting, crushing, sieving, grading, and then mixing with fillers and bitumen in this quarry.

As is generally the case, the high skid-resistance surface chips have to be brought in from a specialized source. Bituminous macadam is transported in insulated 20 tonne loads, which can keep the material warm for 5–10 hours before specialist machinery lays and compacts each layer of the road. Today, typical trunk roads have lane widths of about 4.7 m.

Dean Welburn uses several technical terms to describe the rock processes, most of which are self-explanatory, and it is not vital that you remember them. A 'shaping' machine is a crusher designed to produce equidimensional rather than flattened fragments.

Taking typical values from Table 17, and assuming that the local rock is sufficiently strong for no capping layer to be needed, what is the minimum amount of aggregate needed (in cubic metres) per kilometre of four-lane major road (assume an average porosity of 10%)?

From Table 17 the average thickness of the top four layers is about 0.5 m, of which aggregate forms almost 100% of all but the top 0.05 m.

Therefore, a single square metre of road will require:

$(0.5 \times 0.9) = 0.45 \, \text{m}^3$ (assuming road volume overall is about 90% rock)

A kilometre of four lanes will require:
$4.7 \times 4 \times 1\,000 \times 0.45 = 8\,460 \, \text{m}^3$.

Question 29

How does the above value for a four-lane major road compare with the quantities of aggregate required for a major road and motorway shown in Table 6? Suggest reasons for any differences.

7.5 Physical testing of road aggregates

Aggregates used in macadam roads need to have many of the same features as those needed for concrete aggregates:

1 *Shape* Equidimensional fragments are better than flat ones. Crushed rock aggregates, which are more angular in shape, pack down to give a stronger interlocking texture than the more rounded particles from natural gravels, and so are preferred for roads. However, local gravels may be used for the lower layers, or for roads carrying light loads, if they are available and cheaper than crushed-rock material.

2 *Size* The largest sizes are used for the bottom layers, but even they must be less than 75 mm; the upper layers are made of smaller particles.

3 *Grading* All aggregates should be well graded so they form the densest possible layers when compacted down by heavy rolling equipment.

3 *Density* Rocks with a high porosity are unsuitable because they may shatter by freeze–thaw action. The density of the rock from which the aggregate has been made can be important too. Other things being equal, the denser the aggregate is, the more expensive it is to transport. That is because transport is charged by weight, but material for a road is needed by volume. For example, basalt ($2.9\,\mathrm{t\,m^{-3}}$), can be 10% denser than limestone ($2.6\,\mathrm{t\,m^{-3}}$), and so will be 10% more expensive to transport.

4 *Surface texture* The ability to form a strong bond with bitumen is important. Most rocks will bond well enough with cement, but bitumen needs a rough surface to form a strong bond. Crushed aggregates are generally better in this respect than rounded pebbles from natural gravels. The best rock types for a strong bond with bitumen are those like sandstones, quartzites and igneous rocks; the worst are smooth rocks like flint. Because of the demanding conditions suffered by aggregates in flexible roads, a series of special British Standard tests is used to measure aggregate properties for the different layers of a road.

5 *Crushing strength* Aggregates for all layers in a road must have a high crushing strength. They should neither crack, nor crush to a powder where fragments touch each other as the loads pass over. Resistance to repeated dynamic loads is needed in roads, rather than the static loading of the simple crushing test used for concrete, and so a more severe test is required. The most widely used laboratory test for this is a dynamic crushing test, which measures the **aggregate impact value (AIV)**. This involves 15 blows of a 14 kg 'hammer' dropped from a height of 380 mm onto small (10 mm) chips of the sample (Figure 46). The amount of fines (< 2.4 mm) produced in the test expressed as a percentage of the original sample material gives the AIV. The *lower* the AIV, the *higher* the strength of the aggregate; for road aggregate, an *AIV less than 20%* is needed.

6 *Resistance to abrasion* It is important that the aggregate on the wearing course has high resistance to abrasion; that is, it must not be easily worn away (eroded) by rubber wheels. The resistance to abrasion is measured in the laboratory by mounting samples of the aggregate under test in a resin to make a 'pad'. This pad is then held against a rotating rubber wheel, under the abrasive action of wet sand for 500 revolutions. At the end of the test the material worn away from the aggregate in the pad is determined by the weight lost by the pad. The **aggregate abrasion value (AAV)** is calculated as a percentage of the aggregate material lost in the test. The *lower* the AAV the *better* the wearing properties; for a good wearing-course aggregate an *AAV less than 14%* is needed (sometimes as low as 10%).

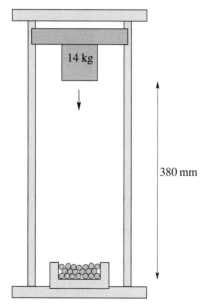

14 kg

380 mm

Figure 46 Aggregate impact value test apparatus. The 'hammer' is shown lifted ready to fall for a blow on to the rock chips in the tray below. After fifteen blows a 2.4 mm sieve is used to remove any small fragments (fines) generated in the test, which are then weighed.

7   *Resistance to polishing*   Some rocks are both strong and resistant to
abrasion, but tend to become smooth and polished if used on a road
surface, allowing vehicles to skid. It is important to have a laboratory test
to measure this. A mounted sample of aggregate similar to that used for
the AAV test is held against a rotating rubber wheel, fed with fine wet
polishing abrasive for a set time. The friction of the polished surface is
then measured in a standard test, in which the swing of a pendulum is
retarded by the friction of the polished surface on a standard pad (Figure
47). This gives the **polished stone value (PSV)** as a percentage. The
higher the value of the PSV, the *better the resistance to polishing*, and
the better the aggregate. For a good wearing course, the *PSV should be
above 60%*, and sometimes values as high as 70% are called for.

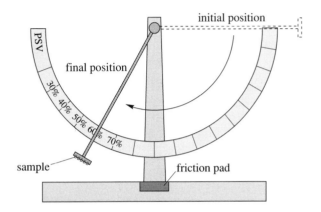

Figure 47   PSV test
apparatus. The friction on the
pad of aggregate limits the
swing of the 'pendulum' in the
test; in this case the PSV = 60.
The smoother the test pad, the
further the swing, and the lower
the PSV of the sample.

The relationship between these three tests for one group of rocks, sandstones,
can be shown in a useful working diagram (Figure 48), on which the results
of all three tests can be plotted. When this is done, the results *for any one
rock* usually fall more or less on top of each other as a single point on this
graph, which makes it a very useful way of comparing a lot of samples and
assessing their comparative suitabilities for use in road-building.

Ideally all aggregates for a road should plot to the lower right of the AIV
20% line, the shaded area. Since few rocks have an AIV of less than 10%,
they will fall into the narrow dark-shaded diagonal area. To make a good
wearing course, aggregate rocks should have an AAV of less than 14, and
PSV of more than 60, and so should fall inside the brown area. (*Note* This
diagram only roughly represents the relationship between the three
properties.)

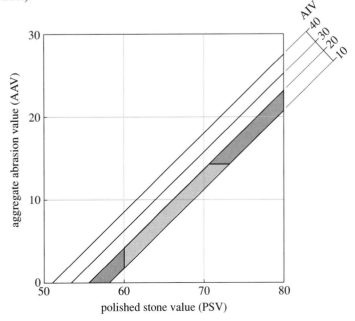

Figure 48   The ranges
in aggregate abrasion value
(AAV), polished stone value
(PSV) and aggregate impact
value (AIV; diagonal axis) for
road aggregates. The coloured
area shows the limiting values of
wearing-course aggregate.

Most igneous and metamorphic rocks are strong enough to have sufficiently low AAVs and AIVs, but often they are easily polished, and so have a PSV value which is too low. This is understandable, since it is igneous and metamorphic rocks which are most widely used as decorative polished slabs (Section 2.6).

The maximum AAV and minimum PSV recommended for wearing-course aggregates or for road surface chippings rolled into the wearing-course asphalt surface, for different road conditions, are given in Table 18. The specifications are very detailed, and seek to balance the amount of traffic using the road and the characteristics of the road itself. Particular emphasis is given to places where friction is most crucial — that is, where traffic has to brake — such as bends and junctions.

Typical test values for several British aggregates are given in Table 19 for comparison.

Table 18 Maximum AAV and minimum PSV for various road conditions

Road type and situation	% of UK roads	Traffic density/ commercial vehicles per lane per day	Maximum AAV for wearing course/%	Minimum PSV for wearing course/%
deceleration lanes on high-speed roads (e.g. approaching traffic lights, and pedestrian crossings)	0.1	<250	14	63–65
		250–750	12	68
		>750	12	70
junctions, roundabouts and bends	4	<250	14	50–55
		250–750	12	55–60
		750–1 750	12	63–65
		>1 750	10	68–70
straight sections of motorways, dual carriageways and trunk roads	15	<1 750	12	55
		1 750–3 250	10	57–65
		>3 250	10	68
minor roads (not deceleration locations)	81	<250	14	50
		250–750	12	53
		750–1 750	12	55–60
		>1 750	10	63–68

Table 19 AIV, AAV and PSV values for some British aggregates

Rock type	Location of quarry	AIV	AAV	PSV
granite	Shap	23	3.5	54
granite	Glensanda	23	4.0	54
'granite'*	Charnwood (Leics.)	10	10	66
basalt	Antrim (N. Ireland)	15	6	57
dolerite (Whin Sill)	Belford (Northumberland)	8	3	57
quartzite	Wrekin (Shrops)	21	5	57
Carboniferous limestone	Derbyshire	23	14	38
flint	Berkshire	23	1	35
coarse sandstone	Yorkshire ('Millstone Grit'†)	29	26	72
arkose‡	Ingleton (Yorks)	11	5	62
'greywacke'‡	Welsh borders	16	9	72

* Not a true granite, but a tough igneous rock, which is often called 'granite' in the aggregate business.

† A coarse-grained sandstone, which has excellent skid resistance, but poor strength, see below.

‡ These are tough recrystallized sandy sediments of Silurian or Ordovician age (pale and dark green on the *Postcard Geological Map*), both often called 'greywacke' or 'gritstone' in the aggregate business. They are widely used for skid-resistant road surfaces.

Many of the properties in Table 19 can be simply explained: the igneous rocks (granite, dolerite and basalt) and the well-cemented silica-rich rocks (quartzite and flint) all have high resistance to abrasion, and so have low AAVs; the first two coarse-grained granites, and the quartzite and flint tend to shatter and so have higher AIVs. The coarse sandstone is not well cemented, and so has AIV and AAV values that are much too high: it will be too easily crushed. The Carboniferous limestone, like all limestones, is composed of the soft mineral, calcite, and so has a high AIV and AAV, but is widely used as aggregate in the lower layers of many roads.

The PSVs are the most revealing, however. Limestone is much too soft and polishes very easily (Figure 49a); flint is very hard, but as it has a very uniform glassy texture, it too develops a very polished surface. The igneous rocks and the quartzite look promising for many wearing-course locations, because, as they are worn away by the traffic, the harder mineral grains wear more slowly than the softer ones, so leaving an uneven upper surface on the aggregate particle (Figure 49b). The highest PSVs are all sandstones, which owe their high values to the presence of angular quartz (sand) grains on their wearing surfaces. The highest value is the poorly cemented coarse sandstone (Millstone Grit), which loses grains and crumbles much too fast to be a roadstone. The last two rock types in the Table are both very well-cemented sandstones, in which the sand grains are held in a matrix containing some softer minerals (feldspar in the arkose, clay minerals, micas and small rock fragments in the greywacke). They are both old (> 400 Ma) and are best described as slightly metamorphosed impure sandstones. They have the optimum combination of hard grains of quartz in a slightly softer matrix, so that grains drop out before they become polished, but not too fast for the aggregate to wear away quickly (Figure 49c).

◯ Compared with the other rocks in Table 19, do these chippings have a high or low place value?

◯ They have a much lower place value. Most of the other rocks in Table 19 are used as low-value bulk aggregates, and are mainly used locally.

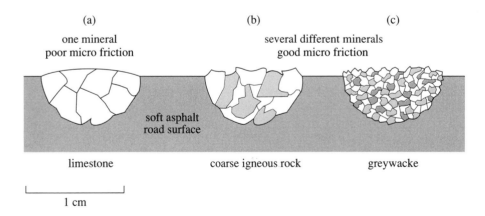

Figure 49 Aggregate fragments in a wearing course asphalt after considerable use: (a) limestone — low PSV; heavily worn, smooth, polished surface (poor macro and micro friction); (b) coarse-grained igneous rock — good PSV; little wear, and irregular top surface maintained by faster erosion of softer mineral grains, leaving harder grains sticking up (good macro and micro friction); (c) greywacke — highest PSV; rough surface of sharp quartz grains is always maintained by slow but constant loss of occasional grains being 'plucked' out by traffic, but the grains are well cemented so that wear is only slow (good macro and excellent micro friction).

PSV is mainly a measure of the micro-scale frictional properties. There is also a macro-scale effect in all cases where chunks of aggregate are sticking out of the road surface, especially when chippings stand proud of softer asphalt (Plate 25b), though clearly this is most effective when the edges of the chipping are not easily rounded off.

With concrete road surfaces, high-PSV materials are generally not used. The surface friction is increased by cutting thin grooves across the road surface at right-angles to the traffic flow, making these roads very noisy to drive on.

Question 30

(a)   On what proportion of UK roads would the Derbyshire Carboniferous limestone be suitable as a wearing-course aggregate, and why?

(b)   On which UK roads could Leicestershire granite be used as a wearing-coarse aggregate?

Activity 8   Audio Band 4   The Rock Kit samples as potential aggregates

This tape applies some of the information on physical properties of aggregates to the samples in the Rock Kit, by applying qualitative tests. You should write your own observations in the last three columns of Table 20. First note the following points on the tests.

Aggregate Impact Value (AIV)   Resistance to splitting (crushing strength), can be tested by gentle 'hammering' between two bricks, to give terms such as: 'very strong', 'strong', weak', 'very weak'. Also try to scratch the samples with the sharp point of the nail in the Rock Kit, to see if any of the grains can be dislodged, or are themselves soft enough to crumble under pressure.

(However you 'attack' your samples, be careful not to expose your eyes to any flying rock fragments, as particles from hard rocks, especially ones like flint, can be very dangerous.)

Aggregate abrasion value (AAV)   Resistance to abrasion can be tested by rubbing each sample in turn on a piece of coarse carborundum paper (silicon carbide) to see how fast they wear away. Silicon carbide is harder than quartz, so even the hardest rocks can be 'worn' in this way. If you devise some 'standard' test of your own, you can give a sort of AAV value to each, even if it is only by terms such as: 'very good, 'good', 'poor', 'very poor'.

Polished stone value (PSV)   This is more tricky. If the sample has grains that keep falling out, it will have a high value, and if there is only one mineral present it will give a low value. The appearance and feel of the surface after rubbing with the carborundum paper may give you some clues.

Some of the information in Table 19 should be helpful here; the values for Carboniferous limestone and flint have been taken from there to start you off.

Listen to the tape now, filling in Table 20 (Question 31) as you go.

Audio Band 4   The Rock Kit samples as potential aggregates

Speaker
Dave Williams Open University

Question 31

Fill in the last three columns in Table 20, using the information above, and the data in Table 19. Note down comparative observations in descriptive terms, rather than numerical values.

Table 20 Aggregate tests on the Rock Kit samples

Rock	Colour	Crystals or grains Size/mm	Minerals	AIV	AAV	PSV
granite	speckled pink	crystals/2–4 mm	quartz, feldspar, mica			
basalt	black	crystals/<0.5 mm	too small			
Jurassic limestone	buff	rounded grains/0.5–1 mm	calcite			
Carboniferous limestone	dark grey	grains/ up to 1 mm	calcite	23	14	38
Permian sandstone	pink	grains/0.5–1 mm	quartz			
Ordovician quartzite	grey/pink	crystals/up to 1 mm	quartz			
Cambrian slate	dark grey	too fine	too small			
Cretaceous flint	brown	glassy	too small	23	1	35

Question 32

(a)   Which three samples would be least suitable for basecourse aggregate?

(b)   Which three of the samples in the Rock Kit might make the most suitable wearing-course aggregate for a stretch of major road?

7.6   Regional distribution of wearing-course aggregates

Although the bulk of aggregates for fill, concrete, and the lower layers of flexible roads still comes from essentially local sources, the demand for higher-specification materials for modern roads has led to some materials being transported great distances. This is particularly so with high-PSV chippings, which command a premium price of up to £50 per tonne.

The best British wearing-course aggregates are those from the Midlands, Welsh borders and North of England, as well as Wales and Scotland, where there are igneous rocks, or sandstones older than 400 Ma, which have been toughened by cementation and recrystallization when buried to great depth.

Generally igneous rocks such as basalt have a fairly high PSV because they are made up of several minerals of different hardnesses, which wear to form an uneven surface (Figure 49b). However, basaltic rocks need to be fairly coarse grained (>0.5 mm, like the dolerite of the Whin Sill at Belford) because fine-grained basalts polish too easily. Most of the younger rocks from south-east England are either too soft (limestones), polish much too easily (flint) or are poorly cemented sandstones, which are not able to resist wear.

Figure 50 shows that the distribution of high-PSV rocks suitable for wearing-course aggregates in mainland Britain is largely confined to the older rocks to the north and west, whereas the chief demand for such materials is in the south-east of the country, where most people live.

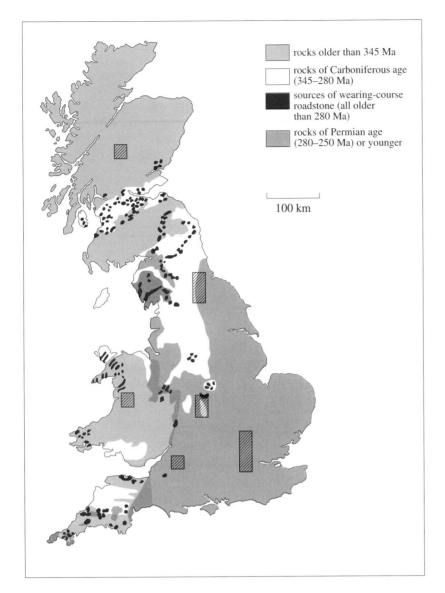

Figure 50 Distribution of rocks suitable for wearing-course aggregates in mainland Britain, and the ages of the rocks. The relative demand for these aggregates is shown by the height of the columns for four areas of England — south-east, south-west, midlands and north — and also for Wales and Scotland.

In early 1992 a new quarry was opened at Leahill on the north side of Bantry Bay near the southern tip of Ireland, to work a hard sandstone with a high PSV, making it suitable as a wearing-course aggregate.

⬤ Is this rock of similar age to the other preferred high-PSV sandstones quarried for wearing-course aggregates on the mainland?

⬤ According to the *Postcard Geological Map*, the rocks there (dark brown) are Devonian in age (345–395 Ma), a little younger than the sandstones worked for high-PSV stone on the mainland.

The intention is to ship this premium road aggregate to markets in the UK, particularly the London area, and continental Europe, especially Germany and Denmark. An initial capacity of around 500 000 tonnes per year is planned to increase to 1.2 million tonnes a year by the mid-1990s, and could be 2 million tonnes a year by the beginning of the twenty-first century.

Question 33

(a)   How can it be economic to open a new aggregate quarry when there is virtually no local market for aggregates?

(b)   Given the planned output, is it likely that most of this stone will be used for the wearing courses of UK and mainland European roads?

A high PSV may not be essential for many purposes, but if its other properties are suitable, a high PSV is never a disadvantage. If this Irish rock can be delivered cheaply to markets that need large tonnages of aggregate, then it could be economic.

Question 34

Many Victorian streets were covered with blocks of granite or similar igneous rocks that have worn well for many years. Even if it were feasible to pave motorways in a similar way, why would this be unwise?

Activity 9

Find out what materials are used for the high-friction surface chips on the main roads in your area.

Comment   In the north-east of England, dark fine-grained chips are likely to be basalt or dolerite, such as is found in the Whin Sill (Video Band 5); pink chips are very fine-grained granitic rock from the Cheviots or dark sandstone or 'gritstone' (sometimes called greywacke) from the Scottish borders. In southern England, similar gritty rocks come from the Welsh border (Plate 24b), whereas lighter-coloured and coarser materials are likely to be igneous rocks (Plate 25b), such as granite from Leicestershire. On roads carrying little traffic, you may find a lower-quality local material.

If you are able to collect the odd fragment, it may be that your tutor will be able to identify it at the next tutorial.

7.7   Summary of Section 7

1   Crushed-rock aggregates are now consumed in larger quantities than the traditional sands and gravels, and are used largely in concrete and road construction, where their high crushing strength is an advantage.

2   Aggregates for concrete-making must have fragments of a mixture of sizes, they must be well-graded in the engineering sense, so that they pack down to give a strong, low-porosity mass.

3   A rock for crushing to make aggregate should itself be of a low porosity to prevent frost damage, and free of particles that react chemically with cement.

4   Aggregates for roads must have a high crushing strength, measured as its aggregate impact value (AIV) in a dynamic test.

5   Aggregates or chippings on a road surface must have resistance to abrasion, measured as the aggregate abrasion value (AAV), and have high friction, measured as the polished stone value (PSV).

6   High-PSV aggregates are not available in many places in the UK, and so some aggregate has to be brought long distances, especially to the south-east of England.

8 FUTURE AGGREGATE SUPPLIES

This Section is a brief introduction to the much wider issues that relate to the present and future supply of aggregates. As the industry moves from local to regional, national and even international markets, quarries get bigger, the capital investment involved increases enormously, and the question of how much aggregate is extracted, and from where, becomes much more complex. There are often articles in the press about quarrying, which are usually at least as much to do with politics as with the geology and economics of aggregate supplies.

Now watch the whole of Video Band 5: *Rocks for Roads*, the final section of which considers aggregate supplies for the future.

Video Band 5   Rocks for Roads

Speakers

Eric Dack	Blue Circle Cement (quarry manager, Eastgate)
Ross Dunn	Blue Circle Cement (general manager, Dunbar)
Alan Ruxton	Blue Circle Cement (quarry manager, Dunbar)
Dean Welburn	RMC Roadstone (Technical Manager, Belford)
Ian Wilson	independent consultant (a pioneer of the superquarry concept since the 1970s)
Murray Morton	Chairman of RAGE (Residents Against Gravel Extraction), Egham

Apart from the details of the individual quarries, there is a larger issue running through Video Band 5. While viewing the programme, consider the question: 'where are we to get our aggregates for the future, and at what cost to the environment?' Although the two limestone quarries at Eastgate and Dunbar are not being worked for aggregate, they are both large limestone quarries, and in that respect not untypical of many Carboniferous limestone aggregate quarries.

8.1 Aggregate supplies and environmental issues

Since our demand for aggregate far outstrips all our other quarrying needs, it is in the area of aggregate that issues of supply and the environment most frequently occur. Many of the traditional quarrying areas lie in the National Parks or in areas of outstanding natural beauty, but of low employment opportunities. In places such as the Yorkshire Dales, the Peak District of Derbyshire, and the Mendips south of Bristol, rocks like the Carboniferous limestone have been worked for many years. As demand has increased over the years, many of the quarries have become very large, working beds of limestone up to 100 m thick, and making large scars in the local scenery.

The conflicting demands of future aggregate need and the desire to preserve the scenery of such areas for recreational use, presents difficult choices. This is made more so as demand for aggregate increases. At the same time, efficient, modern quarrying methods involve higher capital investment in fewer larger quarries.

This is the first environmental issue: *location of the rock to be quarried, and the market to be supplied.*

Question 35

If a 30 m thick bed of horizontal limestone is being quarried to produce 600 000 t of aggregate a year, what area of quarry is worked out each year, assuming the rock has a density in the ground of $2.5 \, t \, m^{-3}$?

Question 35 shows that the land needed each year for quite a medium-sized quarry is extensive, and can result in a large hole if quarrying goes on for many years. In an area where there are many quarries the impact on scenery can become important, so today restoration is always considered before planning permission is given for a new quarry. Since all sedimentary rocks occur in beds of limited thickness, it is not possible to minimize the visual impact just by quarrying deeper. Nor is it always possible just to open a quarry elsewhere, because a suitable rock may not be available. At the consumption rate of crushed-rock aggregate in the early 1990s, the UK needs the equivalent of 250 quarries of this size to supply our requirements (Figure 15).

Transport can be a contentious issue for large quarries, especially if the output has to be sent out by road.

Question 36

Imagine that the quarry sent all its output in standard 201t lorry loads through an adjacent village. How frequently would vehicles pass through the village if there was only one way out of the quarry in Question 35, assuming 250 working days a year and an 8-hour working day?

No wonder the local inhabitants sometimes complain.

This highlights the second environmental issue: the *method of transporting* the aggregate to market. Some of the larger inland quarries deliver much of their material from the quarry in special trains, which can take up to 3 000 t in a single shipment. This not only has a dramatic effect on the local environmental impact of the quarry operations by reducing road traffic, but, because rail is inherently cheaper, it also enables the aggregate to be supplied to markets much further afield (see transport costs in Table 4).

In addition to the issues of location and transport of the aggregate, there is the whole question of the perceived impacts on the local area — positive in terms of jobs created, but negative in terms of noise and disruption.

The third major issue is therefore that of *environmental impact* and the *viability or sustainability* of the quarrying operation in the future.

This is the most difficult area to discuss because it includes matters such as:

(a) *Demand* for the quarry output and the continued economic viability of the quarry in a changing external business environment of competing supplies, changing markets, changing transport costs, etc.

(b) *Local planning issues*, such as the attitudes of the local planning authority, politicians, and local population.

(c) *National issues*, such as the need for supplies of aggregate for major schemes such as road-building and coastal defences, and the impact of government policy on *sustainability and recycling*.

(d) *International issues*, such as EU environmental policy on quarrying, pollution, etc. Aggregate is now internationally traded, and so the *supply and demand on the international aggregate market* are also becoming important.

8.2   Quarries, planning and NIMBY

In Section 7.6 we noted that there was a marked regional imbalance between the supply and demand for high-PSV aggregate for surfacing roads (Figure 50). But as this is for the road surface layer only, the amounts of material involved are rather small. Once large volumes of building materials have to be carried long distances, there are two quite separate problems: the cost of transportation, and the planning issue of where the material is to come from, often called the NIMBY syndrome (not in my back yard).

Murray Moreton put it nicely in Video Band 5, when he asserted that in the Egham area three-quarters of the back yard had *already* been dug up for sands and gravels! The implication was that it was time to dig elsewhere.

If building materials are extracted to meet a local demand, then there is a fair chance that the conflicting interests of the extractors and the users of the resource, on the one hand, and the local inhabitants who live near the quarries on the other, can be settled at a local level using the planning machinery run by the county councils. County councils, as the planning authority, keep an up-to-date plan of land available for aggregate working for their area, within the framework of a local land bank. Planning for future supplies of building materials is clearly an important local issue, as we saw in the Northamptonshire example at the end of Section 3. But what happens when the scale of the quarrying is very large, and the demand is not just a local one?

8.3   From local quarries to superquarries

Any large-scale extractive industry inevitably causes some local disruption, and often transport of the rock itself can be a major irritant, especially if road transport is used on minor roads. When supplies of aggregate from one part of the country are in demand on a large scale in another region, the problems become more tricky. If aggregate is to be transported long distances, then to make the operation economic, it has to be carried out on a large scale; that implies large-output quarries. Large quarries are intensively mechanized, and once expensive machinery has been installed it has to be kept running to service the capital costs of its purchase and installation.

For some years the appetite of the south-east of England for aggregates has far outstripped the supply from the local sand and gravel pits, and has increasingly been met by crushed-rock from quarries in the south-west and the Midlands. Already there are several huge quarries with outputs of over a million tonnes a year, and a few of about 5 million tonnes. These inland quarries, with their major markets up to 150 km away, make a custom-designed transport system such as special trains a possibility, and Figure 51 shows the pattern of transport by rail which brings aggregates from the south-west and Leicestershire to the south-east. Similarly, some aggregate is taken to the north-west from Derbyshire and North Wales, though mostly by road.

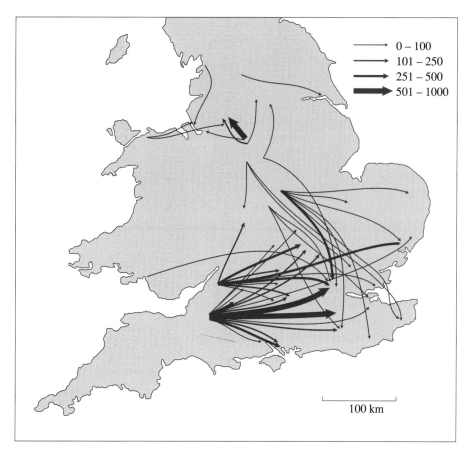

Figure 51 Major rail movements of crushed rock aggregates from inland quarries in England and Wales in the late 1980s. Figures quoted are in thousands of tonnes per year.

○ Use the *Postcard Geological Map* to try to identify the main rocks being exploited as aggregates for the south-east in Figure 51.

○ This is tricky, because the outcrops of the rocks concerned are very small on the map. Most of the rock from the south-west comes from two areas of (pale brown) Carboniferous limestone, one in the Mendips, south of Bristol, and the other north of Bristol. The area in Leicestershire is a very small (purple) spot, which represents an area of granite and volcanic rocks, surrounded by Triassic rocks, which are widely quarried for aggregate around Charnwood.

But just as the local sand and gravel workings in the Thames valley have become inadequate to meet local demand, how sustainable is the present pattern of supply, with a handful of these large quarries, supplying aggregate to distant markets? Should this be the pattern for the future, with an ever-increasing demand to be met? Some would argue that enough of the 'back yard' of scenic areas of Carboniferous limestone in the Mendips, the Peak District and the Pennines has already been taken. The pressure on the Mendips is clear from Figure 51. It is against this background that the coastal superquarry idea was born.

8.3.1 Coastal superquarries and sea transport

Now read the article *Super-quarries* by Robert Muir Wood.

Note on terms used:
Glensanda is on the north shore of Loch Linnhe, which runs north-east from Oban and Mull.
The granite is shown as a large red mass on the *Postcard Geological Map* on the north-west of the Loch.
Portlandian (170 Ma), *Eocene* (50 Ma), *Dinantian* (340 Ma) and *Liassic* (190 Ma), are all ages of rocks.
Mtpy = millions of tonnes per year.   *Caledonian* is another rock age, about 400 Ma.   *Biotite* is black mica.

EARTHWORKS

SUPER-QUARRIES

Robert Muir Wood

Time was, if you wanted building stone, you simply dug a hole next to the construction site. In the mountains of northern Pakistan, a geologist with whom I was working discovered that villagers would rather build unstable house-walls from nearby rounded cobbles than carry angular blocks from 500 m away. In many parts of Europe where farms and simple houses were built from the local stone, one can still map geology from changes in the indigenous building material. Cathedrals might deceive, proclaiming Portlandian when bedrock was Eocene; but in a farmhouse, Dinantian or Liassic reflected the local subcrop.

In Europe the situation changed in the 19th Century. The introduction of the railway allowed distant quarries to supply every-day needs, yet no building-stone proved as cheap as its mass-produced brick or concrete imitation. For the history of quarrying is 1% geology and 99% transport economics. As long as every stone was carried by horse or hand, every village had a quarry. Quarries became fewer and larger as transport costs diminished. The new transport arteries: canals, railways and roads, all demanded quarried stone for their construction, and better transport then allowed fewer larger quarries to become concentrated at more distant locations. Yet even these quarries had problems coping with the great demand fluctuations of building and civil engineering. When demand was slack quarries closed. By the time the market improved the machinery was rusted, the labour force dispersed and the owners bankrupted. Starting up new quarries encountered environmental and planning problems that might take years to overcome. Yet quarrying was such an unglamorous, basic activity that little imagination was given by quarry owners to outlining some more strategic future.

While the economics of road and rail transportation have undergone no

dramatic changes in the past few decades, a transport revolution has occurred at sea. Todays price differential per kilometre is staggering. Weight for weight, transport by sea costs 3% that of rail and 0.5% that of road. Discounting loading and unloading costs, for a bulk cargo, it is cheaper to ship material to Rotterdam from New York than freight it by road from The Hague. It is for this reason that European coal mining is on its knees: ocean-going bulk carriers have turned the world into a single mineral market-place, even for the cheapest commodities.

In 1976 a British Government sponsored report, with the catchy title: 'Aggregates; the way ahead' proposed a strategic innovation: the creation of coastal super-quarries, large enough to survive demand fluctuations, able to take advantage of the transportation savings of shipping.

The first European operator to follow this lead was Foster Yeoman, an English family owned company, started in the 1920s with a bulldozer, a dumptruck, and a small hole in the ground. Foster Yeoman is already operator of the largest single producing quarry in Europe, at Torr in south-west England where 7.8 Mtpy of tough Carboniferous limestone is sold to the prosperous but stone-poor southern and south-east England. Recognizing that quarrying is all about transportation Foster Yeoman is the only private company to run its own locomotives (American giants) on the state-owned British railway system. Foster Yeoman now has a new ambition: by the year 2000 it intends to operate the largest super-quarry in the world.

After prospecting for a suitable location the company bought a mountain on the wild west coast of northern Scotland in 1981. The mountain is made out of a Caledonian age intrusion of hard tough pink biotite granite, located next to deep water, sufficiently far from national parks or major communities that planning restrictions seemed unlikely

to be an obstacle in development. Glensanda was more than 10 km from the nearest road, and Foster Yeoman chose to sustain this isolation, preferring to supply the site by ship or (for key personnel) through a small airstrip and a six-seater airplane. This isolation caused some unforeseen problems for the project: secrecy generated local suspicion and on a weekend in early 1989 the expensive equipment at the isolated site was sabotaged and burnt by extremist Scottish nationalists. The issue was less one of an English company exporting the very fabric of Scotland than that the whole prospect was taken to be a covert attempt to construct a nuclear waste repository.

With the attention focussed on their transport budget Foster Yeoman recognized that a major cost in quarry operation comes from the need to drag stone up to the surface. The 500 m high mountain site was ideal for planning an alternative strategy in which the work of raising the rock had already been exerted by tectonic processes during the Tertiary. Gravity shifts the stone, through a 'glory-hole' at the centre of the pit.

The site measures 1000 m by 1300 m; the glory hole (blasted in early 1988) is 3.8 m in diameter and falls 280 m where it joins a 1.8 km long conveyor tunnel which passes to the shoreline storage area. Construction work in the last year has been focussed on eight rock-cut storage bins, each 17.5 m deep, with a total capacity of 0.5 Mt. These in turn feed into a conveyor system on a ship-loader which can fill 70,000 t of granite

EARTHWORKS

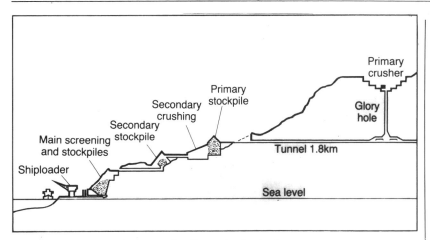

Schematic view of the super-quarry in Glensanda, Scotland.

aggregate into a ship's hold in 24 hours. Without any need for underwater rock-blasting Panamax class bulk carriers with 70,000 ton capacity can approach close enough to the natural rocky shoreline to be loaded.

All the equipment at the site has to be designed to withstand the abrasive wear from granite: 100 ton capacity dump-trucks have been fitted with thick rubber bodies. In one hours treatment of 800 tons of granite, 1 mm of manganese steel is worn from the central gyratory of the rock crusher. The project has so far cost more than £25 million with an additional £45 million of investment planned for the 1990s. In 1989 it was intended to produce 4.5 Mt of granite, rising to 12–15 Mt per annum in 1995 and 20 Mtpy by 2000.

At present the principal market for the aggregate lies in south-east England and the surrounding fringes of the southern North Sea: 1.4 Mt of both fine and coarse Glensanda aggregates are being used in the concrete linings for the Channel Tunnel. The main depôt for the product is on the Isle of Grain, in the outer Thames Estuary, 70 km east of London.

The quarry is already undergoing its first test: the present recession in the British building industry, accompanied by high interest rates, would be enough to turn many medium sized quarries into water-sports centres. Already Glensanda has had to lay off a significant proportion of its 300 workforce, but its future is becoming assured through supplying international markets.

Every month 1 Mt of shipping travels empty between Europe and North America: bulk carrier holds filled with 40,000 tons of ballast water for the journey west. By adding only 72 hours to their European turn-rounds bulk carriers can now sail to Glensanda and then on to Houston where 70,000 tons of granite is unloaded in 4 days. A 15 year deal has now been signed to take advantage of this surplus capacity, so that as Europe burns coal from Utah, so Texas will build with granite from Scotland.

Other super-quarries are now being planned. One is already in operation in Nova Scotia, supplying 10 Mtpy of crushed rock. By the early 21st Century, having put most of their smaller rivals out of business, there will be a regional, even global, pricing and supply battle amongst a few super-quarries. Geologists planning a career in the aggregate industry of the future would do well to concentrate their minds on transport economics, rather than igneous petrology. In fact, there will probably be almost no careers: a handful of super-quarry geologists could probably advise on production for the whole of the European market. Yet keep watching the oil price: sooner or later digging the bedrock from a hole in the back-garden may once again become cheaper than importing it from western Scotland.

Question 37 _____

What are the main developments that have made the concept of coastal superquarries a viable alternative to inland quarries for large-scale aggregate production?

Question 38 _____

What are the important similarities between the Glensanda operation today and the export of the Erquy Red Beds from Erquy to South Wales in the last century?

8.3.2 Coastal superquarries in the future

One of the key issues for the future of aggregate supplies is the balance to be struck between local small-scale sand and gravel pits (thousands of tonnes a year), regional crushed-rock quarries (up to a million tonnes a year), very large inland quarries, like those now supplying the London area (1–5 million tonnes a year), and the establishment of new coastal superquarries (>5 million tonnes a year).

Undoubtedly a cluster of coastal superquarries could eventually relieve the pressure on inland sites, thereby 'exporting' the NIMBY issue away from the centres of population.

Glensanda is not the only coastal superquarry in the world (see article by Robert Muir Wood), but it was the only one operating in the UK in the early 1990s. However, in 1993 permission was sought to open a new superquarry at Rodel on the island of Harris in the Hebrides. The location of the superquarry is in another igneous intrusion (a white rock, rich in feldspar, called anorthosite). Initially, the local council was in favour, but here also there were strong local protests. The Secretary of State for Scotland called in the plans, and ordered a public inquiry, which sat from October 1994 to June 1995. In early 1994, preliminary proposals were made for another coastal quarry on Harris at Loch Seaforth to work gneiss. There have also been proposals to work limestone and gneiss further north on the Scottish mainland at Durness, which has generated a local action group to oppose the scheme.

A report that investigated potential sites for superquarries around the Scottish coast has showed that several more could be considered suitable on geological grounds: there is no shortage of crystalline rock adjacent to deep-water berths (Figure 52); see also p. 17 in *The Geological Map* booklet.

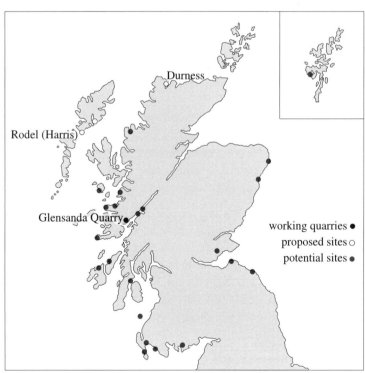

Figure 52 Some potential coastal superquarry sites in Scotland, a preliminary survey based largely on the geological suitability of the rock.

In 1994 the Department of the Environment (for England) issued a new planning document: *Guidelines for Aggregate Provision in England* (MPG 6), HMSO, April 1994. This indicated:

> that by 2011 demand for aggregates provision in England and Wales could rise to between 370–440 Mt per year, and that in the 20 years to 2011 about 6 000–6 500 Mt of aggregate in total could be needed for England alone. [England is assumed to account for about 90% of total UK demand.] (para 22)

> that in line with the principles of sustainable development, there should be less reliance on traditional primary land won sources of aggregates …which should reduce from 83% to 74% by 2001 and 68% by 2006. (paras 25, 26)

> that subject to tests of environmental acceptability an increasing level of supply can be obtained from coastal superquarries…It is unlikely, however, that [these] potential sources will contribute greatly to the demand in the first 10 years. (para 44)

At the same time the Environment Department of the Scottish Office issued its own national planning policy guideline: *Land for Mineral Working* (NPPG 4), Scottish Office, April, 1994. Here it is stated that:

> On the basis of previous geological and technical research, the Government believes it would be reasonable to constrain superquarry numbers [including Glensanda] to an upper limit of 4 in the period to 2009…and that these should be geographically dispersed. (para 64)

> Given the existing development at Glensanda…that suitable sites for superquarries may be found on the north coast of the Highland Region, in the Shetland Islands and in the Western Isles. (para 67)

> Also, besides coastal superquarries [defined as ones with an output of at least 5 Mt per year], the Secretary of State…wishes to be notified of all coastal quarry proposals with a planned extraction of 2 million tonnes per annum or more which the planning authority is minded to approve. (para 69).

Thus a framework has been created for the future in which coastal super-quarries are seen from England as a source of 'an increasing level of supply', while from Scotland only 'up to three more' are likely to be allowed, and these in widely dispersed locations. The scene is therefore set for a major planning and environmental debate to develop well into the next century.

The UK is already importing large blocks of Norwegian gneiss for coastal defence work. Staithes on the Cleveland coast has a breakwater of Norwegian gneiss, and, just north of Spurn Point on the Humber estuary, large volumes of this rock are being imported to protect an important North Sea gas terminal plant built near the edge of an eroding cliff. On a smaller scale, 5 000 tonne loads of ERB were being taken by boat in 1994 from the Erquy area to Jersey for harbour construction (Plate 26).

Meanwhile, a major UK aggregate company announced in May 1994 that they had acquired the right to develop a coastal superquarry at Jossingfjord, south of Stavanger, in another anorthosite intrusion, and were aiming to supply the European coastline including the UK market with material from Norway using 70 000 tonne ships. This is a very favourable location, considerably nearer to many of the major European ports than Scotland.

The export routes for Scottish, Irish and Norwegian rock are shown on Figure 53. It seems that the day of the coastal superquarry has arrived; the question is how many will there be, and where will they be sited.

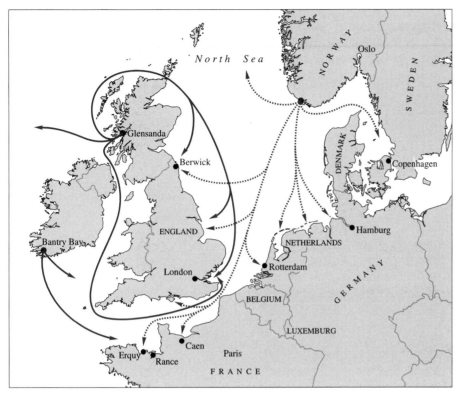

Figure 53 Superquarry export routes from Scotland, Ireland and Norway.

It is likely that other superquarries are at the advanced planning stage. What is new for the future is that there will be aggressive competition for aggregate markets *internationally*, and if the aggregate from coastal superquarries can be delivered to where it is needed more cheaply than from older inland quarries, the superquarries will win. Large projects on the coast like the Channel tunnel, barrages across estuaries, coastal airports, and coastal defence work are all ideal markets for coastal superquarries because they can deliver directly to the site by sea.

8.4 Sustainability: reclamation and recycling

It has been suggested that as it becomes more difficult to obtain permission to open new quarries, and to extend existing quarries in the UK due to the increased sensitivity about all 'environmental' issues, perhaps a more appropriate acronym than NIMBY would be 'BANAANAAA' (Ban any new activity anywhere near anyone at all).

If we produce over 200 million tonnes of building materials (largely aggregate) each year, where does it all go? It isn't 'consumed' as we consume coal or oil, it is not exported, so it must still be here somewhere. Good masonry stone is valuable, and so is recycled when a building is demolished. Traditionally, old buildings were knocked down and new ones erected on the rubble of the old. In many cities, the present ground level is a metre or so above the mediaeval ground surface, with the Roman level lower still, and much of this is due to the accumulation of old building materials.

Today, old bricks and concrete usually end up as builders' rubble or hard core, and much of it is dumped to waste, often in the very quarries from which new building materials had been extracted previously! Some road-building material is recycled, but the construction industry is generally geared up to using freshly dug aggregates. In some cases the standard specifications that control the composition of building materials do not allow for a significant element of recycled material. 'Over-specification' and safety-first 'over-engineering' also militate against the conservation of new materials and the recycling of old building materials. Given the huge amounts of building materials that have been extracted over the last 30 years, and the large stockpiles of quarry and mine wastes, there must be considerable scope for more recycling of these materials as pressure grows for a more sustainable approach to developments.

As to future changes, it is likely that there will be an increasing demand for the greater recycling of materials such as building wastes, especially hard core, for re-use as aggregates, but at the moment large-scale re-use of this material is not economic. It has been suggested that the wastes like sand from the china clay industry in Cornwall could be used in a Severn barrage, but some form of subsidized transport would be needed to make it competitive against supplies from coastal superquarries. There are also huge supplies of coal shale in old tips, as well as PFA, burgy, etc., all potentially recyclable to some extent, which could be used instead of freshly quarried aggregate. It is possible that future EU pollution and recycling legislation may discourage tipping of potentially recyclable materials by, for example, imposing a 'disposal levy'.

Another development could be levies imposed on 'virgin' resources, to actively encourage recycling, and it is very likely that legislation may further control the impact that future quarries are allowed to make on the local environment, on both inland and coastal sites, but it seems likely that the coastal quarry is here to stay. The sheer volumes of material that can be efficiently quarried and crushed in remote locations, and then cheaply delivered to coastal locations in the heart of north-west Europe and the USA, effectively gives these ports their own hard-rock quarries if only they can find a deep-water quayside location to unload the large ships.

If recycling does become a more important part of UK or EU policy, low-cost aggregates will not necessarily be among the first materials to feel the impact of legislation. There are probably larger economic benefits from the recycling of domestic and industrial wastes, containing much higher-value materials: metals, glass, paper and plastics, most of which presently goes to landfill.

8.5 Summary of Section 8

1 Aggregate is no longer a cheap material readily available locally all over the country.

2 The trend for the supply of high-quality aggregates has been towards fewer large inland quarries with outputs in the range 1–5 million tonnes.

3 The perceived environmental disturbance caused by aggregate quarrying is becoming a major factor limiting the opening of new quarries; the NIMBY attitude is now a major factor in the exploitation of aggregates.

4 Recently, coastal superquarries have begun to operate in Scotland, Norway and Nova Scotia, and rock from these quarries is now being supplied to distant coastal markets.

5 Even intercontinental shipment of aggregates has been shown to be feasible with ships of 70 000 tonnes.

6 Future pressure for a more sustainable approach to resource exploitation is likely to lead to the greater use of recycled building materials.

OBJECTIVES

Now that you have completed Block 2, you should be able to do the following:

1   Explain in your own words, and use correctly, the terms in the Glossary relating to Block 2.

2   Perform calculations involving tonnages and volumes of building materials, and relate these to areas and volumes of quarries on the ground.

3   Explain the different categories of building materials, and how their properties are utilized in different types of construction.

4   Explain the importance of place value for building materials, and how this varies for different modes of transport.

5   Describe the distribution of building materials in the UK in terms of their ages, as shown on the *Postcard Geological Map*.

6   Describe the desirable properties of natural building stones, including the term 'freestone'.

7   Relate the properties of the samples in the Rock Kit to the properties of large masses of rock used for construction purposes.

8   Explain the origin of sands and gravels being formed today, and relate these to similar materials formed during recent glacial periods.

9   Explain the processes whereby loose sediments are transformed into hard sedimentary rocks.

10 Relate the properties of clay minerals to the brick-making process.

11 Explain the importance of limestones for the cement industry.

12 Relate the formation and properties of gypsum to the processes of evaporation and precipitation.

13 Relate the properties that make some rocks sought after as the raw material for crushed-rock aggregates to their distribution in the UK on the *Postcard Geological Map*.

14 Relate the properties that can be measured by laboratory tests on rock samples to those needed by aggregates used to make roads.

15 Discuss in your own words the concept of sustainability as applied to building materials.

16 Analyse the reasons why there is a trend in the aggregates business from small local sand and gravel pits, to fewer larger hard-rock quarries, and then to giant coastal superquarries.

ANSWERS TO QUESTIONS

Question 1

(a)   In the early 1990s, building materials production in the UK was 250 million tonnes per year. As the UK population is about 55 million, per capita UK production was about: $250 \times 10^6/55 \times 10^6 = 4.5\,t$ per annum.

(b)   Per capita world production was about $20 \times 10^9/5.5 \times 10^9 = 3.6\,t$ per annum.

So the UK was about 25% above the world average in per capita production.

Question 2

Table 21   (Completed Table 2) Amounts of materials in jar (column 5 Table 1)

Materials	30 mm onions	14 mm onions	7.5 mm peas	3 mm rice
number	8	104	450	5 440
volume/cm^3	210	175	120	100
total volume of particles/cm^3	605	605	605	605
volume, as % of total volume of particles	35	29	20	16

(a)   See Figure 54.

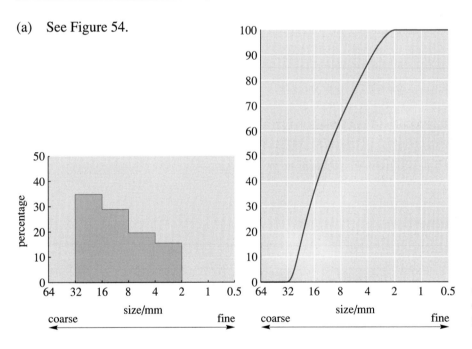

Figure 54   Completed Figure 4g and 4h with results plotted from Table 21.

(b)   The pickles in the jar are coarser-grained than the sediment in Figure 4d since they plot to the left of the other data (note the different scales in Figure 4).

(c)   The pickles are better sorted than the sediment in Figure 4f because they have a smaller range of grain sizes, and so plot as a steeper line on the graph.

Question 3

(a)   London lies on rocks of Tertiary and Pleistocene age (up to 65 Ma), and Dublin on rocks of Carboniferous age (280–345 Ma), so the rocks under London will be about 250–300 Ma younger than those under Dublin. Rocks below London are described as 'clays and sands'. They are very young, and so are unlikely to be well cemented. The older Carboniferous 'limestones and sandstones' under Dublin are much more likely to be suitable for building stone.

(b)   The Cretaceous outcrop curves around London in a V-shape because these rocks form a large downfold, a **syncline**, called the London Basin. Strata to the north of London dip to the south-east, and the same strata south of London dip to the north. (There is a useful sketch of the London Basin on p. 26 of *The Geological Map* booklet.)

(c)   The pale brown represents Carboniferous (280–345 Ma); the dark brown represents the older Devonian (345–395 Ma). Since the older rocks surround the younger, this must be another syncline; it is in fact the 'basin' of the South Wales Coalfield. (There are sketches of the northern and southern parts of this basin on p. 22 of *The Geological Map* booklet, and on p. 18 there is a map and cross-section of a similar basin in Scotland.)

(d) (i)   200 Ma is about the age of the *youngest* Triassic (195–230 Ma), so it must be almost at the *top* of the Triassic; it lies about 23 mm (160 km) north of London, near Leicester (see p. 25 of *The Geological Map* booklet).

(ii)   300 Ma is near the top of the Carboniferous (280–345 Ma), about 35 mm (250 km) north of London, in Derbyshire or south Yorkshire.

(iii)   400 Ma is almost at the top of the Silurian (395–445 Ma), about 65 mm (460 km) north of London, just about at the Scottish border.

(iv)   There are two (bright red) outcrops of igneous rock about 400 km and 430 km north of London. They are labelled 'intrusive', and so must be *younger* than the surrounding pale brown Carboniferous strata. Therefore they must be younger than about 300–350 Ma. In fact, these outcrops are part of a sheet of basaltic rock, the Whin Sill, of which you have a sample in the Rock Kit, and which runs across the north of England to the Farne islands. (See also p. 19 of *The Geological Map* booklet and Video Band 5: *Rocks for Roads*, which visits an aggregate quarry in the Whin Sill.)

Question 4

(a)   Many of the buildings showed evidence of the stone having been split across the original sedimentary layering; also hand splitting and guillotining of the ERB in the mason's yard to make small pavement slabs showed the ease with which the rock could be cut to size in any direction. The polished slabs showed no sign of regular flaws. All these are characteristics of a freestone — that is, one that can be split or cut equally easily in any direction.

(b)   They are formed chiefly of the mineral quartz (SiO_2), which is a hard mineral, resistant to wear. The rock is a metamorphic rock, and so has a recrystallized texture, forming a very tough, hard-wearing material, ideal for cobbles. This also makes it a good rock for cutting and polishing: the grains do not drop out during polishing.

(c)   The quarry was next to a port, so cobble stones could be cheaply transported. Coming back from South Wales the boats were full of coal, so useful cargo was carried both ways.

Question 5

(a)   Assume a 20 tonne load of the cheapest crushed rock (£3 per tonne):

quarry gate cost = 20 × £3 = £60

transport cost = £0.1 per tonne per km,
or £20 × 0.1 = £2 per km per load

The transport cost will be equal to the cost of the rock, £60, after 60/2
    = 30 km

For any greater distance, transport costs would exceed quarry gate costs.

(b)   Value of 10 tonnes of the cheapest slates = $10 \times £400 = £4\,000$ per 10-tonne load.

The transport costs (if we assume the same cost per km for a half as a full load):

$$= £20 \times 0.1 = £2 \text{ per km per load}$$

Therefore, transport costs would exceed the on-site value after

$$\frac{4\,000}{2} = 2\,000 \text{ km}$$

Question 6

(a)   See Figure 55. The area worked out approximates to two 'blocks', one about $600\,\text{m} \times 250\,\text{m} = 150\,000\,\text{m}^2$, the other approximately $150\,\text{m} \times 150\,\text{m} = 22\,500\,\text{m}^2$. Assuming that the area unworked between Byfield and Firs mines is about the same area as that unworked to the north-east outside the rectangles, the total area is approximately $172\,500\,\text{m}^2$, or 17.25 hectares.

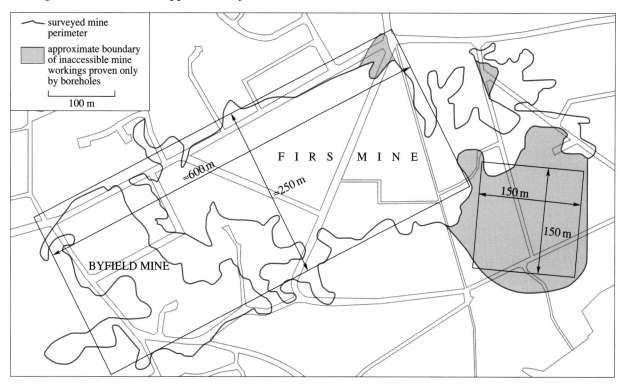

(b)   Volume to be filled: $172\,500\,\text{m}^2 \times 2.5\,\text{m} = 431\,250\,\text{m}^3$.

Therefore, the weight of grout to fill the mined area:

$$= 431\,250\,\text{m}^3 \times 2\,\text{t m}^{-3} = 862\,500\,\text{t}$$

So nearly a million tonnes of grout would be needed.

Figure 55 Old limestone mines beneath Bath: worked-out area.

Question 7

(a) 10^6 tonnes of rock will occupy:

$$\frac{10^6\,\text{t}}{2.5\,\text{t m}^{-3}} = 400\,000\,\text{m}^3$$

(b)   The depth of the hole will be: (volume of rock/area of quarry):

$$\frac{400\,000\,\text{m}^3}{5\,000\,\text{m}^2} = 80\,\text{m}$$

So, the area of a football field would have to be excavated to a depth of 80 m to yield a million tonnes of rock.

Question 8

(a) Area of the quarry face $= 20\,\text{m} \times 50\,\text{m} = 1\,000\,\text{m}^2$.

Therefore cutting back the quarry face 1 m will yield:

$1\,000\,\text{m}^2 \times 1\,\text{m} = 1\,000\,\text{m}^3$, that is, $1\,000\,\text{m}^3 \times 2.5\,\text{t}\,\text{m}^{-3} = 2\,500\,\text{t}$ of rock

1989 output in the UK was about 300 million tonnes (Figure 14), so the face would have to be advanced:

$$\frac{300 \times 10^6}{2\,500} = 120\,000\,\text{m} \equiv 120\,\text{km}$$

(b) If the face advances 120 km per year, it will come towards your house at:

$120 \times 1\,000\,\text{m}/365\,\text{days} = 329\,\text{m per day}$; or $329/24 = 13.7\,\text{m per hour}$

Question 9

In 1965 (see Figure 15) much more sand and gravel (100 million tonnes) was produced for aggregates than crushed rock (70 million tonnes); by 1975 about 115 million tonnes of each were produced. In 1985 the balance had shifted to 115 million tonnes of crushed rock, and to just over 100 million tonnes for sands and gravels. This gap seems to be widening, because although production in 1991 of both was down from their peaks in 1989, 50% more crushed rock (150 million tonnes) than sands and gravels (90 million tonnes) was produced.

Question 10

the houses will require $10\,000 \times 50 = 500\,000\,\text{t}$
the major roads will require: $12 \times 7\,500 = 90\,000\,\text{t}$
the motorway link will require: $8 \times 100\,000 = 800\,000\,\text{t}$
total: $1\,390\,000\,\text{t}$

Question 11

Chalk is a soft, porous rock, made of calcite, which is very easily broken down by weathering, and soft Chalk pebbles are easily destroyed when transported in rivers. Flint, being very tough, is highly resistant to weathering and erosion, and so survives river transport.

Question 12

See Table 22 (completed Table 8).

(a) Only in the centre of the face, beneath holes A and C is the gravel worth extracting (more than 3 tonnes of gravel for each tonne of overburden).

(b) According to the values in Table 22, there are $1\,500\,\text{t}$ worth extracting within the given overburden ratio (that is, the blocks of ground below A and C). In practice, the 700 t below B would be taken too, because the overburden ratio for blocks A–C as a whole is better than 1 : 3. The pit would probably not be extended to line E–H unless richer material became available beyond this line.

Table 22 Logs for boreholes shown in Figure 19, overburden ratios, and tonnages of gravel present

Depths in boreholes/ m	A	B	C	D	E	F	G	H
(a) to top of gravels	1.0	1.5	1.0	1.5	0.5	1.0	2.0	1.0
(b) to bottom of gravels	4.5	5.0	5.0	2.5	1.5	2.5	3.0	3.5
(c) thickness of gravels/m (b − a)	3.5	3.5	4.0	1.0	1.0	1.5	1.0	2.5
(d) overburden : gravel ratio (a : c)	1 : 3.5	1 : 2.3	1 : 4	1 : 0.7	1 : 2	1 : 1.5	1 : 0.5	1 : 2.5
(e) economic? (yes or no)	yes	no	yes	no	no	no	no	no
(f) weight of gravel in 10 m × 10 m column ($= c \times 10 \times 10 \times 2$)/t	700	700	800	200	200	300	200	500

Question 13

(a)   See Table 23.

Table 23   Results of two trial borings in 'area of search'

Logs of boreholes*	Trial boring A	Trial boring B
height of ground above sea-level/m	160	120
water-table/m	none found	7
topsoil/m	0–0.3	0–0.2
boulder clay/m	0.3–4.4	0.2–0.6
glacial sand and gravel/m	4.4–7.4	0.6–7.4
solid rock/m	7.4	7.4
average sand and gravel composition:		
fines(< 0.06 mm)	31%	16%
sand(0.06 –4 mm)	46%	49%
gravel (4–64 mm)	23%	35%
sand and gravel thickness/m	3.0	6.8
overburden : sand and gravel ratio	1 : 0.68 (4.4 : 3)	1 : 11.3 (0.6 : 6.8)

* Depths in boreholes are given in metres below ground surface.

(b)   B has a much more favourable overburden to sand and gravel ratio (of about 1 : 11). A has an overburden to sand and gravel ratio of 1 : 0.68; there is less sand and gravel than overburden, so A is not economic.

(c)   B is the more promising because it has only about half the amount of fines that A has; these fines will have to be washed out.

(d)   Water is present in B, which could mean flooded workings. But as the water table is almost at the bottom of the sand and gravel, this is unlikely to be a real problem.

Question 14

(a)   There is unlikely to be an abundant supply of brick clay in areas of the country underlain by rocks older than the Carboniferous, namely much of Scotland, Wales and south-west England, because these rocks have been altered by metamorphism and many of the original clay minerals will have been destroyed.

(b)   Superficial deposits are generally fairly thin and variable, and so provide smaller and less uniform resources as a basis for a large-scale extractive industry than thick beds of clay rocks in the stratigraphic column.

Question 15

(a)   One brick is 240 mm long and the wall is built to a height of 20 bricks. Thus, 8×10^9 bricks will make a wall

$$\frac{8 \times 10^9}{20} \times 0.24 \, \text{m long} = \frac{8 \times 10^9}{20} \times \frac{0.24}{10^3} \, \text{km}$$

$$= 0.096 \times 10^6 \, \text{km}$$

$$\approx 96 \times 10^3 \, \text{km}$$

which is enough to go more than twice around the Equator!

(b)   Using the value for brick production in 1990 from Figure 26b, the volume of bricks produced in 1990:

$$= 4 \times 10^9 \times 0.22 \times 0.1 \times 0.075 \, \text{m}^3 = 6.6 \times 10^6 \, \text{m}^3$$

Therefore, the area of pit needed each year:

$$= \frac{6\,600\,000}{20}\,\mathrm{m^2} = 0.33 \times 10^6\,\mathrm{m^2}$$

a third of a square kilometre, or an area about the size of 60 football pitches.

Question 16

(a)   Volume of clay: $100\,000\,\mathrm{m} \times 25\,000\,\mathrm{m} \times 20\,\mathrm{m} \times 30\% = 15 \times 10^9\,\mathrm{m^3}$
(15 *billion* cubic metres).

(b)   Volume of clay needed for 1.2 billion bricks (30% of 1990 production indicated in Figure 26b):

$$= \frac{1.2 \times 10^9}{400} = 3.00 \times 10^6\,\mathrm{m^3}$$

Therefore, years of reserves:

$$= \frac{15 \times 10^9\,\mathrm{m^3}}{3.00 \times 10^6\,\mathrm{m^3}\ \mathrm{per\ year}} = 5\,000\ \mathrm{years}$$

Question 17

(a)   Subsidence is unlikely on sandy soils because these soils are not subject to appreciable compaction when they dry out, since the grains are already firmly in contact with each other (like the loose sand shown in Figure 6b).

(b)   The clays younger than about 55 Ma, such as the London Clay, are most susceptible to shrinkage because they contain a high proportion of the clay mineral montmorillonite, which contains the most water in its structure (Figure 25). In fact, houses built on the London Clay are the most susceptible. However, some of the very youngest clays, ball clays, are rich in kaolinite, and so are less vulnerable.

(c)   The London Clay (pale buff on the *Postcard Geological Map*) is especially likely to cause subsidence problems, because it occupies such a large area in the built-up centre of the London Basin.

Question 18

(a)   One million, because that is what MN, 'meganewton', means (10^6 newtons).

(b)   Half of the crushing strength:

$\dfrac{40}{2}\,\mathrm{MN\,m^{-2}} = 20\,\mathrm{MN\,m^{-2}} = 20 \times 10^6\,\mathrm{N\,m^{-2}}$. This would be produced by:

$2 \times 10^6\,\mathrm{kg} = 2 \times 10^3\,\mathrm{t} = 2\,000\,\mathrm{t}$ acting on an area of $1\,\mathrm{m^2}$. So:

$2\,000\,\mathrm{t}$ of granite can be supported on $1\,\mathrm{m^2}$.

$1\,\mathrm{m^3}$ of granite weighs 2.6 t. Therefore a column height of $2\,000/2.6 = 769\,\mathrm{m}$ of granite could be supported on the plinth before half the crushing strength was exceeded.

Question 19

(a)   3 months is about 100 days, by which time the compression strength is $40\,\mathrm{MN\,m^{-2}}$ (Figure 37a).

(b)   Tricalcium silicate (a little) and dicalcium silicate (mainly) are responsible for the increase in strength (Figure 37b).

(c)   According to Figure 37a, full compressive strength of about $44\,\mathrm{MN\,m^{-2}}$ is reached some time after 3 years, probably nearer 5 or 8 years.

Question 20

(a)   See Table 24.

Table 24   Brick and cement production 1960 to 1990

	1960	1970	1980	1990	Fall in production 1960–90	% fall in production 1960–90
no. of bricks/10^9	7.2	6.1	4.6	3.8	3.4	47
wt of cement/10^6 t	13.6	17.2	14.1	13.6	0	0
ratio 10^9 bricks : 10^6 t cement	0.53	0.35	0.33	0.28		

(b)   See completed bottom row. The output of bricks relative to cement has fallen during each decade, indicating that substitution has occurred. By 1990 the ratio had fallen by almost a half from the 1960 value (0.53 to 0.28).

(c)   See completed final two columns. Yes, it is clear that although between 1960 and 1990 brick production fell by 47%, cement production did not fall at all.

Question 21

(a)   Cement blocks are the cheapest, by the tonne, and even more so by the cubic metre (see Table 25). Aggregate cannot be used to make a wall, nor is concrete suitable, as it requires expensive formers to hold it while it cures.

Table 25   Comparative costs of building materials (local retail prices, late 1992)

Material	Cost	Cost/£ t^{-1}	Density/t m^{-3}	Cost/£ m^{-3}
common bricks	£15 per 100	65	1.7	111
facing bricks	£20 per 100	86	1.75	151
hand-made bricks	£45 per 100	193	1.8	347
cement blocks (= 6 bricks)	£42 per 100	33	1.3	43
lightweight (insulated) blocks (= 6 bricks)	£65 per 100	135	0.5	69
aggregate or sand	—	20	2	40
cement	£3.60 for 50 kg	72	not relevant	not relevant
readymix concrete	—	24	2	48

(b)   Not necessarily, because the better insulation from lightweight blocks (less than half the density of the normal cement blocks) will save on fuel costs in the long run.

Question 22

(a)   Imagine a 'column' of seawater 1 m² in area and 100 m deep. It will contain water weighing 100 t, which will have dissolved in it 3.5 t (3.5%) of salts, of which 78.04% will be NaCl (Table 15).

Therefore, weight of NaCl:

$$= 3.5 \times \frac{78.04}{100} \, t = 2.73 \, t$$

If this has a density of $2\,000\,kg\,m^{-3}$ ($\equiv 2\,t\,m^{-3}$), it will form a layer:

$$\frac{2.73}{2} \, m = 1.36 \, m \text{ thick}$$

(b)   Similarly for gypsum, the water column will contain $3.5 \times \dfrac{3.48}{100}$ t of gypsum (density $2\,t\,m^{-3}$), which will form a layer:

$$\left(\frac{3.5 \times 3.48}{100} \times \frac{1}{2} \right) m = 0.061 \, m \text{ thick}$$

Question 23

(i)   See Figure 56.

(ii)   Gypsum is much more abundant in the columns in Figures 42b and c (15–25%) than the column in Figure 42a (3.5%). This is because in nature there are likely to be long periods of the earlier stages of evaporation (80–90% water loss) when mainly gypsum is being precipitated (Figure 41).

(iii)   Common salt, NaCl, and the most soluble magnesium and potasium salts are less abundant in nature than indicated in Figure 42a, because these will only be precipitated in the later stages of evaporation (NaCl) or when it is almost complete (potassium and magnesium salts), a very rare event in nature. In addition, even if complete evaporation were to occur, these very soluble salts are likely to be redissolved subsequently by the next influx of the sea.

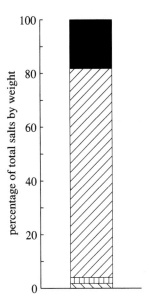

Figure 56   The completed Figure 42a. The amount of calcium carbonate has been exaggerated so that it can be seen; it should be only 0.33%.

Question 24

Sugar is very soluble in water. So when drops of water are added to sugar a lot of sugar can dissolve. When the water evaporates, the dissolved sugar recrystallizes, cementing the grains together.

Gypsum, by contrast, is very *insoluble* in water. Table 15 shows that gypsum forms only about 3.48% of the 3.5% by weight of dissolved salts in seawater, so that normal seawater contains only about 0.12% of dissolved gypsum. Figure 41 shows that this begins to precipitate when the seawater has shrunk to 19% of its original volume. At this point the concentration of gypsum in seawater must have increased about five times — that is, to about 0.6%. So the small percentage of water used to mix the plaster can only have dissolved the minutest amount of gypsum. The mechanism for hardening the plaster cannot be solution and precipitation like the sugar, but involves the formation of hydrated calcium sulphate (gypsum) from hemihydrate; see Equation 6.1.

Question 25

There are several possibilities:

- the increased demand for aggregates as more building is done with concrete;
- shortage of supply due to sterilization (building over) of sand and gravel deposits;
- environmental pressures making planning permissions more difficult;
- requirement for high-strength aggregates for advanced civil engineering projects.

Question 26

(a)   See bottom line of Table 26.

Table 26   Building materials weighed wet and dry to estimate porosity

	Engineering brick	Common brick	FBA cement block	Lightweight block	Concrete	Limestone A	Limestone B
(a) dry wt/kg	3.45	2.34	0.30	0.385	0.600	1.10	1.31
(b) wt after water immersion for 20 min./kg	3.45	2.53	0.325	0.40	0.605	1.14	1.30
(c) gain in wt/kg	0	0.19	0.025	0.015	0.005	0.04	0.01
(d) gain in wt/%	0	8.1	8.3	3.9	0.8	3.5	0.8
(e) density/t m^{-3}	2.0	1.7	1.3	0.5	2.0	2.6	2.6
(f) porosity/% of dry volume	0	13.8	10.8	1.9	1.7	9.5	2.0

(b)   The lowest porosity is the engineering brick (0%); the highest is the common brick (13.8%).

(c)   Limestone A, with its much higher porosity (9.5%), would probably suffer more frost damage than limestone B (porosity 2.0%), and so limestone B is better for the garden wall.

Question 27

The slate and the sandstone. The slate would split into flat fragments, which are the wrong shape to pack down to give a low-porosity aggregate. The sandstone is very poorly cemented, and is friable, with a low crushing strength, and so would not be suitable for making high-strength concrete. It is also a porous rock, likely to suffer frost damage.

Question 28

(a)   The sandstone, because it is made of quartz grains and so would make a high micro-scale friction material. However, it is poorly cemented, and so might wear rather fast. It is not clear from a small sample whether it would split into slabs suitable for paving stones. In fact it is used to make large paving stones as well as a building stone (Plate 12) in the Penrith area.

(b)   The granite and the basalt are both igneous rocks, and are therefore likely to have the high crushing strengths needed for kerbstones; both have been widely used (Plate 14). The ERB sample is also suitable, and this rock is known to have been widely used for this very purpose (Figure 9b).

Question 29

The values in Table 6 (tonnes per km) are: major road, 7 500; motorway, 100 000.

Our calculations showed that 1 kilometre of four-lane major road requires 8 460 m^3 of aggregate. At a density of, say, 2.5 t m^{-3}, this is equivalent to 8 460 × 2.5 = 21 150 t, a value that lies between those in Table 6 for major roads and motorways. It is likely that the A1 is built to a standard somewhat higher than the average major road in Table 6, and the A1 has four lanes.

A motorway normally has six lanes, as well as two hard shoulders, and a central divider, so can be expected to require at least twice as much per kilometre as the A1, that is, about 42 300 t km^{-1}. The motorway figure in Table 6 is more than twice as big as this, which could be accounted for by the extra material needed for bridges, interchanges, etc., on motorways, and for a capping layer and perhaps a thicker sub-base layer.

Question 30

(a)   None, because although it has an AAV of 14 (Table 19), which is acceptable for a number of low traffic density situations, its AIV is rather too high at over 20%. The real problem, however, is the PSV of 38, which is well below the minimum level of 50, for the least busy roads.

(b)   With very low AAV and AIV of 10 and 10, the only limitation will be the PSV of 66. This is acceptable for most motorway and major roads, except the most heavily used junctions, crossings and deceleration lanes, which form a very small part of the whole road system.

Question 31

See Table 27. (Some numerical values have also been included here, although you are not expected to have been able to estimate them from your sample.)

Table 27 Aggregate tests on the Rock Kit samples

Rock	Colour	Crystals or grains Size/mm	Minerals	AIV	AAV	PSV
granite	speckled pink	crystals/2–4 mm	quartz, feldspar, mica	very strong [23	good 3.5	good 54]
basalt	black	crystals/< 0.5 mm	too small	very strong [8	good 3	good 57]
Jurassic limestone	buff	grains/0.5–1 mm	calcite	very weak 40?	very poor 30?	very poor 40?†
Carboniferous limestone	dark grey	grains/up to 1 mm	calcite	strong [23	poor 14	poor 38]
Permian sandstone	pink	grains/0.5–1 mm	quartz	very weak, crumbly 60?	very poor 25?	very good 70?
Ordovician quartzite	grey/pink	crystals/up to 1 mm	quartz	strong 20?	very good 3?	good 60?
Cambrian slate	dark grey	too fine	too small	weak 30?	very poor 25?	very poor 40?
Cretaceous flint	brown	glassy	too small	strong [23	very good 1	very poor 35]

* Numbers in square brackets are taken from similar rocks in Table 19.

† Numbers with a ? after them are rough estimates from the tests in Audio Band 4.

Question 32

(a) The sandstone, because it is soft, has a very high AIV and AAV and is very porous; the slate which is weak and has a tendency to split into flat plate-like particles, would not consolidate to a dense mass, and the Jurassic limestone, which is fairly soft and porous, and has a high AIV and AAV.

(b) The three candidates are the granite, basalt and quartzite. The limestones, sandstone and slate are either too weak (AIV) or too soft (AAV) or both, whereas the flint, though strong enough, has a very low PSV.

Question 33

(a) The remote coastal location indicates that the output will go directly into ships, which are by far the cheapest method of transport for long distances.

(b) With huge tonnages being planned, it is likely that the rock will be delivered to European ports at a price that may well make it competitive for other uses besides roads. Only a small fraction of the aggregate for a road needs a high PSV.

Question 34

Using granite sets in cities was ideal for slow horse-drawn traffic, where macro-friction was important. On a motorway, granite blocks would become polished by modern high-speed traffic, and so offer much less resistance to skidding than a modern road surface, where high-PSV chippings have high friction properties on a micro scale.

Question 35

$600\,000\,\text{t}$ occupy $\dfrac{600\,000}{2.5}\,\text{m}^3 = 240\,000\,\text{m}^3$

As the bed is 30 m thick, the area worked will be:

$$\frac{240\,000}{30} = 8\,000\,\text{m}^2$$

that is, an area approximately 100 m by 80 m, which is almost a hectare $(10\,000\,\text{m}^2)$.

Question 36

A quarry producing $600\,000\,\text{t}$ a year would involve $600\,000/20 = 30\,000$ truck loads.

If there are 250 working days in a year, this represents $30\,000/250 = 120$ loads of rock out a day.

But each truck comes back empty, so in an 8-hour day there will be:

$$\frac{120 \times 2}{8} = 30 \text{ passes per hour}$$

or on average, one every 2 minutes.

Question 37

The single most important factor is the availability of large ships (up to $70\,000\,\text{t}$), which are by far the cheapest way to move bulk materials including aggregates. Once at sea, the transport costs are so low that very distant markets like the USA can be supplied. A subsidiary factor is the increasing difficulty in obtaining planning permission for very large inland quarries, and the high costs of transporting aggregates overland.

Question 38

One of the advantages of the ERB–South Wales stone trade was that the ships were filled with coal from Wales for the return trip, so the transport costs were halved. Similarly, the same ships that now bring cheap coal across the Atlantic to the UK could return, in principle, with Glensanda granite as a ballast that is also an economic cargo; again the transport costs must be much lower with the ships full in both directions.

Acknowledgements

The author would like to thank the Block Assessor, Geoff Browning, of Staffordshire University, for his helpful comments and for information on waste disposal, and Graham Smith and Ian Wilson for information on Scottish quarrying.

The following student readers are thanked for their comments on an early draft: Tom Denne, Julia Adamson and Iris Rowbotham.

Grateful acknowledgement is made to the following sources for permission to reproduce material in this text:

Text

R. Muir Wood, 'Super-Quarries', in *TERRA Nova*, **2** (1990), 1, pp. 91–2, Blackwell Scientific Publications Ltd.

Figures

Cover: Satellite composite view of Earth, copyright © 1990 Tom Van Sant/ The GeoSphere® Project, Santa Monica, California, with assistance from NOAA, NASA, EYES ON EARTH, technical direction Lloyd Van Warren, source data derived from NOAA/TIROS-N Series Satellites; all rights reserved; *Figure 2a:* Spectrum Colour Library; *Figure 2b:* Dr Olwen Williams-Thorpe; *Figure 9b and c:* Studio Leveque, Erquy; *Figures 11 and 55:* M. T. Froggatt, *Stone Mines at Combe Down*, Bath City Council; *Figures 14 and 15:* G. J. Lofty, D. E. Highley *et al.*, *United Kingdom Minerals Yearbook 1991*, British Geological Survey (1992); reproduced by permission of the Director, British Geological Survey; NERC copyright reserved; *Figure 16a:* reprinted from A. Berger, *Vista in Astronomy*, **24** (1980), p. 103; copyright " 1980 , with kind permission from Elsevier Science Ltd, The Boulevard, Langford lane, Kidlington, OX5 1GB. UK; *Figure 21a:* M. J. Kendrick, 'The proposal maps', *Northamptonshire Minerals Local Plan 1991–2006: Deposit Draft*, Northamptonshire County Council (1993); *Figure 21b:* K. J. O'Shaughnessy, *Nene Valley Management Plan: Background and Strategy*, Northamptonshire County Council (1985); *Figure 22:* Naomi Williams; *Figure 24:* adapted from Table 1 in M. Fields and L. D. Swindale, 'Chemical weathering of silicates in soil formation', *New Zealand Journal of Science and Technology*, **36** (1954), Sect. B, 104–54; *Figure 25:* adapted from G. D. Hobson (ed.) *Developments in Petroleum Geology, Part II*, Applied Science Publishers (1980); *Figure 28:* Don McPhee, *The Guardian*, 16 January 1993; *Figure 32:* Aerofilms; *Figure 33:* R. M. Wood *On The Rocks*, BBC Publications (1978) *Figure 34c:* reproduced by permission of the Director, British Geological Survey; NERC copyright reserved; *Figure 35:* Devon County Council; *Figure 36a:* Aalborg Portland Cement; *Figure 36b:* D. D. Double *et al.*, 'The hydration of Portland cement', *Proc. Roy. Soc.*, **359** (1978), 435–51; *Figure 36c:* H. F. W. Taylor, 'Portland cement: hydration products', *Journal of Educational Modules for Materials Science and Engineering*, **3** (1981), no. 3; *Figure 38:* P. Grimshaw, 'Blue Circle's Dunbar quarry is different', *International Cement Review*, April 1992, Tradeship Publications Ltd; *Figure 40:* Beamish North of England Open Air Museum; *Figure 41:* B. J. Skinner, *Earth Resources*, 2nd edn (1976); copyright " 1976, reprinted by permission of Prentice–Hall, Inc., Englewood Cliffs, N. J.; *Figure 42:* H. Borchert and R. O. Muir, *Salt Deposits: The Origin, Metamorphism and Deformation of Evaporites*, Van Nostrand Reinhold (1964); *Figure 48:* J. R. Hawkes and J. R. Hosking, *Quarry Managers Journal*, February 1973; reproduced by permission of the Director, British Geological Survey; NERC copyright reserved; *Figure 51: Aggregates: The Way Ahead*, Report of the Advisory Committe on Aggregates, Department of the Environment (1975); " Crown Copyright, reproduced with the permission of the Controller of Her Majesty's Stationery Office; *Figure 52:* I. Wilson and C. D. Gribble, *Report on the Potential for a Large Coastal Quarry in Scotland*, Department of the Environment (1980); " Crown Copyright, reproduced with the permission of the Controller of Her Majesty's Stationery Office.

Course contents

This text is one of the components of the Open University course S268
Physical Resources and Environment. The titles of the Blocks of the
Course are:

Block 1: *Physical Resources — an Introduction*

Block 2: *Building Materials*

Block 3: *Water Resources*

Block 4: *Energy 1 — Fossil Fuels*

Block 4: *Energy 2 — Nuclear and Alternatives*

Block 5: *Metals 1 — Ore Deposits*

Block 5: *Metals 2 — Resource Exploitation*

Block 6: *Topics and Data*